HOW TO THINK FAST
ON YOUR FEET
(WITHOUT PUTTING THEM IN YOUR MOUTH)
FOR THE BUSINESS PROFESSIONAL
WHO DOESN'T KNOW WHAT TO SAY WHEN ...

Cherie Kerr

Illustrations by: Molly Peach

Permissions Department, ExecuProv, DePietro Performance Center
809 N. Main Street, Santa Ana, CA 92701

ExecuProv Press

Printed in the United States of America

First Edition

ISBN #:0-9648882-8-9

For:

Cameron, Brendan, Tianna
and
The one that we have been waiting for.

May each of you remain fearless and fast….

ACKNOWLEDGMENTS

I owe a deep debt of gratitude to those hundreds of ExecuProv students who ripped off their ties and kicked off their high heels throwing caution to the wind as they willingly took part in the Fast On Your Feet class. Though they were scared witless, their quest to become fearless and fast truly inspired me. I commend each of them for their bravery and their hard work.

Thanks to my children Shannon, Drake and Keith and my grandchildren, Cameron, Brendan, Tianna and the little one on the way. They are the most precious of all God's blessings and they continue to inspire me to help others.

The concept of friendship takes on even more meaning as each year goes by with the "girls." Carol Ann, Judy, Barbara, Teri, Cathy, Gretchen, Jane, Janet, Ruth, Carol C., Nancy and Sheila.

Mom, it doesn't get easier. You dance in my dreams. Dad, the echo of your string bass lives in my soul. I just need to turn off the world and close my eyes to hear it.

Mokes, no one makes me laugh harder. Thanks for the ice plant. Keep it comin'.

Appreciation to all my friends at my alma mater, the L.A. Groundlings, and also to all those who I have taught and directed at the Orange County Crazies. Every one of you has enlightened me in your own special way.

How To Think Fast On Your Feet

(Without Putting Them In Your Mouth)
For The Business Professional
Who Doesn't Know What To Say When ...

Table of Contents

*"I changed my mind, Mason, forget the report on the bottom line. Intro-
duce next year's projections."*

INTRODUCTION

IF THE SHOE DOESN'T FIT:
When It Turns Out The Way You Didn't Plan It

...so, Steve is seated at the conference room table—confident and upbeat—campaign ideas in hand. He tilts them upward to present the restaurant advertising concepts to Rachel, his client. She suddenly asks, "Who came up with these: Dan Quayle? Geez, you can't even spell...potato." Steve's mouth moves but no sound comes out. He stares at the mockups with her. He then zeroes in on the one with the hash browns. He's speechless.

Then there's Candy. She's rehearsed every one of her opening remarks to address six of the most important meeting planners her hotel has ever brought together in one room. Eagerly, she begins, "I'm so glad you could be here, today, gentlemen. It certainly is a pleasu..." One of them suddenly and inappropriately blurts out, "Hey, Candy, are you married?" Crimson, she says, "Wel ... I .... tha ... uh ... um.... I.... Her words are fragmented—on and off—a verbal strobe light.

How about Brian? "What's that, Mr. Hunter?" he says. Hunter (again), "I *said*, how many of your units fit on a standard pallet?" Brian stares at him attempting to focus. Forget the words, his lips won't even part. His mind just flat-lined; his thoughts abruptly detached from all life support. *What was the answer? Damn*, was all that was left inside his head and that he definitely couldn't utter.

1

And what about Patricia? Her boss sits nearby just to listen in, he says, while *she* conducts the meeting. Patricia: "… so then, if you could all remember to turn in your vacation requests by …" The boss cuts her off, " Turn them in to me first, I need to know whether or not there's any overlapping—oh, sorry, Patricia, go ahead." Patricia continues, "Yes, then … I guess turn them in to Mr. Hodges *first* …" Her boss, now standing, "Make it by the fifteenth because I need to coordinate schedules." And just as Patricia is gearing up to handle another agenda item, he does it once again, reminding those in the meeting to put their requests on the *new* form. He finishes with, "Oh, sorry, Patricia…." Through it all Patricia stops and starts, starts and stops. Her responses are like those of a car shifting from one gear to the next without the benefit of a clutch. A guttural grinding. Soon she's tongue-tied. She's thinking thoughts like: *This would be an excellent time for a tornado … an earthquake … a mudslide … a wayward meteor.* Never mind, she decides. *She's* the natural disaster! Patricia is hopelessly and helplessly unable to respond with an appropriate comment. She's lost her place. Her verbal skills have no motor.

Steve, Candy, Brian and Patricia are not alone. They are like so many other corporate professionals scattered about offices all across America. Though they want to, they simply do not think fast on their feet. Instead, when *it* doesn't turn out the way they planned—whatever the business moment—they clutch, freeze, stall, panic and sometimes just stand there, sputtering or staring.

Like the group above, those unable to respond when they should or want to often leave their respective meetings or business encounters with an angst that hangs on like a nagging head cold. And, yes, like the symptoms of a lingering head cold, the frustration and remorse will eventually dry up and fade away, but the real problem often persists or even worsens. Soon they have developed a habit of clamming up altogether. With enough mental lock downs some folks soon find themselves dealing with a full-blown phobia. Every time they're up against a tense, unpredictable or confrontational situation and can't think of a quick, appropriate response, they feed that phobia. And as they feed it, they chip away at their confidence. Confidence in the way we communicate, especially under pressure, is what we all need in order to be successful on the job, whether we're the mayor of a large city, a retail clerk, a dockworker, a teacher, a sales executive or a high-powered CEO. (God help the auctioneer!)

Often—and I mean *very* often—because we spend so much time *obsessing* over those times when we just couldn't come up with something to say on the spot—we eventually *do* think of the right thing to say … *later*. It could be seconds, minutes, hours or days later. But, unfortunately, it's still later and then it's just *too* late! What some have said is that the perfect corporate comeback usually hit them when they were in the shower, driving the car, or in the midst of picking out the perfect honeydew. But like the contestant on the game show: The right answer only counts when you answer the question right then and there. Not later.

What's worse, many I coach have told me that in the midst of their horrible *moment of stall* they felt like running from the room screaming out loud, bursting into tears, throwing themselves onto the floor face first, or having to reach for the Imodium AD. (I knew one guy who carried a crumpled brown paper bag in his briefcase so he could stave off his hyperventilation attacks.)

Most of us have had moments like Steve, Candy, Brian and Patricia—times when it turns out the way we *didn't plan it*—and there we are feeling ashamed, embarrassed and frustrated—as we're left holding the proverbial bag, all because we are unable to think *fast*.

Sound familiar? Have you had instances when—without warning—that meeting agenda suddenly shifted; your boss or client flipped positions on you; or out of nowhere, you were unsuspectingly put on the spot? And don't forget the *confrontation*. Ever had one of those on the job? That can be the worst of all unexpected events. For many of us, those moments can literally shut down our brain waves—shock us into mental hypothermia, and there we are: frozen, our tongue stuck to a mental ice cube.

Here's another issue that plagues many: anticipatory thoughts. They often get in the way because anticipating something that *does not* come to fruition can throw you off kilter—that alone can cause you to become verbally immobilized.

Whatever the reason for your hesitation, that few seconds of (or complete) silence may seem like a deafening eternity. During those moments, and for a long time afterwards, your mind is left hopping in endless circles of regret.

Then what?

For many, therapy!

But, the good news is you don't need a mental health professional or communication specialist to pull you out of this communication funk or help you solve this agonizing dilemma. All you really need is a skill set that will empower you when communication situations don't unfold the way you planned. Yes, you *can* learn to be consistently quick, nimble, agile, on top of it all—and appropriate, too!

It doesn't matter who you are, where you work, or what professional position you hold, it's important that you are able to think *fast on your feet*. And this book is all about teaching you how to do just that!

Believe it or not, no matter how many times you have been lost for words—even if your tendency to do so has become a regular thing—you *can* overcome it. This book delves into why it is that we are thrown off and unable to rebound spontaneously and what to do to keep that from happening. It also explores what to do when you *do* say something, but it's the *wrong* thing! Another part of this book's message is to teach you how you *can* be in complete control of the awkward communication situation when you are not the *least bit* in control. Sound contradictory? It's not. You'll see.

These are only a few of the lessons/secrets in the following chapters. There's more! So take heart, you're about to learn what those who take my Fast On Your Feet workshop learn.

As I've already pointed out, everyone who has anything on the line professionally has run into a difficult communication moment at least once or twice, me included. I'll never forget the time I was pitching my company to a group of prospective clients. All of them were high-powered types—presidents of companies with billings in excess of $10 million. They were looking for someone to help them train their respective sales staffs in dealing with difficult people and unexpected communication situations. There I was standing before this elite group lecturing on this very subject: *How to be fast on your feet*. One of them piped up in the middle of my spiel to ask, "Were you ever a Playboy Bunny?" Talk about getting bonked in the head with a left field foul ball! (It's the personal questions I'm not expecting, in the middle of my speech, that knock me off kilter.) "Wel-l-l-l-l." (I extended the word well to stall for time in order to grab onto an appropriate and clever retort). It seemed like it took me forever. It felt like my mind was trying to pull up an Internet service without the benefit of DSL support. I finally said, "No, I wasn't. But ... I've been an Easter Bunny." (There was a faint, sluggish laugh.) Now, had I been *faster on my feet*—delivered my comeback with split-second timing, ease and nonchalance, appearing extremely confident, I probably would have gotten a huge laugh. But timing is everything as they say, and I just didn't deliver my response quickly enough. Instead, I stood there for a four-count (comedy show biz term for four seconds) while groping for something to say. So, yes, I've had my moments, too. We all have.

Most of my students—all business professionals—at first tell me, they are skeptical about their ability to *acquire* quick responses. They're not so sure. Nonsense, I tell them! They can, they have, and so will you. It's a matter of learning new tricks.

The new tricks I'm referring to are techniques you may never have even heard of, if you hadn't picked up this book. So, get ready for a delightful and enlightening experience as you become familiar with the Fast On Your Feet tools.

Here's where it begins: There is a fascinating art form in the realm of theater called improvisational comedy. Those who perform it are masters of letting go during any communication situation as it takes place moment-to-moment on stage. In my opinion, improv comedy players are the most adroit communicators on the planet for they are always in the moment—never ahead, never behind—just in the *now*. It is a basic requirement that they remain continually aware, alert, focused, as well as appropriate with what they say and do in every instance. Another dictum for experienced, seasoned improv comedy players is that they relinquish control as they go about their work, and this is how they remain in control. Again this may sound antithetical, but it's not, which you'll see as you make your way through this book.

In case you're not completely familiar with improvisational

comedy: It is a brand of live comedy whereby the actors take to the stage, are given audience suggestions for an improv game or scene, and perform it without knowing ahead of time what those suggestions or the premise of the scene will be. Perhaps you've been one of the millions of television viewers who have watched the completely improvised show, "Who's Line Is It Anyway?", where the actors field audience suggestions and work them out on live TV. Those actors respond to the suggestions and to one another very quickly. For instance, one improv game might be a quick one-minute commercial. The player is given a random object from an audience member (like a comb), and he may be asked to do a quick info-merical on the product, making it anything *but* a comb. They have to name this product, explain how it works; tell the potential buyer (the audience members) what it will do for them, why they should buy it, what else they'll get with it if they buy it today, and so forth. They may even be asked to announce the product's advertising slogan and sing the jingle. They get no time to prepare anything, they just launch into executing the assignment on the spot! All the information they impart, as they say, is delivered off the cuff, moment-to-moment.

In an improv *scene* (as opposed to an improv *game*), there are usually three to five performers who are given a *who, what, and where* from the audience. For example, there may be three bus drivers at the bus terminal trying to locate the buses they have been assigned to drive that day. Maybe the buses are missing. The actors do a complete scene—a beginning, middle and an end—in a time frame of anywhere from two to five minutes, based on that information. They, of course, will have had no knowledge ahead of time as to what that audience suggestion was to be for that scene. In both instances—the infomercial and the bus drivers scene—the actors complete the assignment with precision, bravado, and without hesitation!

How do they do this? It comes as a result of their diligent study. They learn techniques and run repetitive drills that build mental stamina and strength.

The study of improv comedy is invaluable and, if I had my way, actors and business professionals alike would be mandated to study improv comedy techniques before they took to their respective stages. What the improv player learns and what they acquire in the way of mental skills prepares them completely for *anything* communication-wise. Improvisational skills also help build a very deep personal sense of confidence in one's ability to communicate in any professional setting, including confrontational ones.

Any actor will tell you that improv comedy training is wonderful preparation for handling not only tense auditions, but on-stage flub-ups and navigating through a challenging piece of unexpected communication on stage (e.g. forgetting a line or having another actor drop one, disrupting a familiar cue). Realizing this, you can only imagine how valuable learning some basic improv comedy skills might be to you and how positively it can affect your business life. (And, your personal life, too!)

In my estimation, one of the best parts of participating in the rigors of improvisational comedy study is that it not only prepares you to handle situations you hadn't planned for, it's also really fun and invigorating. Easy for the improv comedy actor, you might be thinking, but not for me. Not true, it can be for you, too. I want you to remember this: The improv comedy actor is no smarter, nor is he or she mentally wired any differently than you are. They are just assiduously trained to handle the *unexpected*, what is *not* planned, and do so quickly, effectively, effortlessly—and *fast*.

So that you better understand the philosophy behind this book, let me explain a bit more about my background working with business professionals and how I've used improv comedy techniques to train them. Since 1983, through my company, ExecuProv, I have been training CEO types in public speaking and one-on-one communication through a number of workshops. The central goal for each of the different classes is to equip the business professional with effective presentation/communication skills and strategies. Naturally, "How To Think Fast On Your Feet (Without Putting Them In Your Mouth)" is one of my students' favorites. It has proven to be a Godsend to many for the drills are intense, but heavily result-oriented. I've studied, performed and directed actors performing improv comedy for more than three decades. Performing improv comedy is like doing mental bunge jumping. Studying and preparing for it is akin to going to mental boot camp. You do a series of intense mental aerobics in that camp. I know of no form of communication more challenging than that of improv comedy, as I've pointed out, for you are 100 percent on the hot seat every single moment you are on stage performing. Doing it can be horrifying at first, yet once you conquer that fear, there is nothing more exhilarating than flinging yourself off that mental cliff.

I have discovered, both as a performer and director of others, that after enough drill and success doing this art form, the improv comedy player finds he or she will always come up with the right thing to say, no matter what is said by others on the stage with them. That's the key for the improv player: accepting that *they will never know what to expect and that they have little or no control over the circumstances they are in, but knowing that they will prevail.* And what happens to these players after enough successes on stage is that they come to trust that there is no improv situation where they cannot respond appropriately no matter how unexpected, unplanned or difficult.

The same will happen for you, too, as you master some of the techniques and mindset of these performers. In the end: You, like them, will come to trust your intuition, instincts and impulses and, just like the highly-skilled and seasoned improv player, you will rarely find yourself at a loss for words!

Dwell on this a second: Business professionals are just like improv comedy actors; no one gives us a script every morning as we start off to participate in our typical business day. For all of us life is very often made up on the spot; it's off the cuff! For example, I have no idea what people are going to say to me, today, so I have no idea what I will say back to them. Do you? Now, in many of our day-to-day business dealings not knowing what will be said is no big deal, nothing major hangs in the balance. But in so many other instances it *is* a big deal. Perhaps our job is on the line, a contract, an important sale, the outcome of a critical business meeting … and what direction the conversation goes or flows can be critical, both to the outcome and to our dignity! That was evident during the snippets of scenarios mentioned at the beginning of this Introduction.

In case you have any lingering doubts about the differences between you and the improv comedy player, here is something else I want you to ponder about how much you have in common: Improv performers work with others they trust and are familiar with—those with whom they feel safe communicating—but they also work with audience suggestions (communication they *can't* anticipate). Often they work onstage with people from the audience who they have never before met and they perform with them in scenes, all of which are done impromptu. As you can only imagine, those circumstances can present a great deal of stress. Many audience members might attempt to upstage the performer or become very disruptive. (Loose cannons we call them!) But they manage. You'll learn to do the same. The only difference between you and the improv comedy actor is that your fellow performers will be colleagues, clients and others in the work force. So then, think of those you come in contact with every day as your fellow performers and your audience members because in actuality they are! And, like the improv comedy actor, you, too, will have similar experiences. You'll have fellow performers and audience members who are *with you* and others who are not—who heckle and challenge you.

Though certain aspects of the study of improvisational comedy are at the heart of this book, I don't want you to misunderstand me. I'm not asking you to be funny like most improv comedy players. What I do want you to have in common with them, however, is to learn to remain keenly **focused, alert, quick and undaunted.** Those are the four skills that they learn early on. For them, the comedy comes later. (Should you want to stretch your comedic side and use your humor muscles as part of your new *Fast* tool kit, however, this book will certainly help you develop that God-given talent, as well.)

As you move forward with the lessons in this book, I'm asking that you trust the process the same way an improvisational actor does on the very first day they show up for class. Believe me, it's scary to them, too, because they know they will be put in situations where their mental reflexes will be constantly tested. For starters, I will instruct you the same way I instruct my improv comedy students: Expect the communication to turn out the way you *didn't* plan it and be willing to relinquish control.

This book is the next best thing to participating in the *Fast On Your Feet* class. You can expect to gain the same skills as those who actually are present during a workshop if you do the assignments I have carefully laid out in each chapter. After enough workout of your mental muscles you, like them, will bulk up—build mental strength—and learn to handle any communication improvisationally. One of my chief goals for you is to learn to communicate without trepidation and with great speed and agility as you become self-assured, bold and fearless.

The contents of this book are culled from the lesson plans I use when teaching actors in *mental boot camp*. They are the same drills I use for my one-day How To Think Fast On Your Feet (Without Putting Them In Your Mouth) workshop. Here are the highlights of what it is you are about to learn:

- Why it seems you *cannot* be fast on your feet
- How to handle pressure with ease and presence
- How to be prepared when you're least prepared
- How to handle the unexpected
- How to be quicker and more nimble
- How to acquire a built-in sense of spontaneity
- How to say the right thing at the right time
- How to quickly recover when you say the wrong thing
- How to feel confident about taking communication risks
- How to stay solid and grounded in spite of communication difficulty
- How to *stay* fast on your feet

In addition to the lessons, I've included real-life case situations (in screenplay format), to illustrate how a person first handled their communication *crisis* and subsequently how they and other Fast-On-Your-Feet classmates came upon finding Fast solutions. I'll ask you to create your own *takes* and re-enactments.

As we move forward to begin your work in becoming fast on your feet, grab pencil and paper (or computer) to work on those assignments I'll be handing out. You can't just read about them. You have to do them because each task is specifically designed to build confidence, sharpen your mental muscles and speed up your thought processes, and ultimately, your ability to respond quickly.

Expect to have fun as you move through the pages of this

book, for it is always my policy (because I went to parochial school) that if you have to learn something new you should have fun doing it.

Get ready to process information differently. Get ready to stop *thinking* so much and just *be*. Get ready to adopt the same mindset as that of the improv comedy player, the mindset that prepares each of them for what to say when ....

"Tell me then, what's the ratio of relativity to the square root of 64 as you're baking a cake at 325 on a sunny day?"

Chapter One

ONE SIZE CAN'T FIT ALL:
Learning to Expect the Unexpected

THE REAL HESITATE LADY – TAKE ONE

INT. HOME FOR SALE

Slow, sweeping pan of gracious/spacious master bedroom, full circle. Carpets beige. Walls white. Ceilings cathedral. Plush furniture. An enthusiastic realtor stands before 40ish, newly divorced stockbroker. Wants to see every property she has. This home is a doozey—her best. Knows exactly what she'll say:

MARLA
(Unable to contain enthusiasm)

… the master bedroom is to die for…. It has two walk in closets …

(Waiting for response. Gets none)
and it has a Jacuzzi tub …

13

WEATHERFORD
(Unimpressed)
Uh-huh.

MARLA

and look over here,
(Runs to other side of room. Throws open oversized cabinet
doors. Sweeps across it like Vanna White)a solid-oak
entertainment center! Isn't it something?

WEATHERFORD

Ah … been there, done that.

MARLA
(Smile droops)

Well …

WEATHERFORD
(Almost yawning)

What else you got?

MARLA
(Stumped)

Wha … uh … else?

FADE TO BLACK

The first lesson in this book is to accept the reality that each
of us has little control, if any, over many things—especially how
verbal communication will play out. Sure, you can pre-write
your side of a conversation—Marla may have tried to do just

that; script something for every feature she was about to point out in that master bedroom. She may have even memorized it —but what about the other person (or persons)? You have no idea what they will say or how they will react. Such was the case with Weatherford.

When we realize that dialogue is as unpredictable as the weather—sometimes calm and sometimes stormy, sometimes clear and sometimes foggy—then we're off to a great start. Letting go of the notion that we can control how most conversations will go, and being willing to stop planning for them to go a particular way, is our starting point in this book.

SEVERAL STEPS AHEAD

Buy into this idea: Whatever conversation you know you're going to have, accept the fact that it's going to be different from what you imagine.

Next, realize this: There is no one way to handle a similar circumstance or situation, for each piece of verbal communication has a "life" of its own. In other words, if you find yourself in a new sales call setting today, selling the same thing you sold yesterday, don't think the dialogue is going to be (or should it be) the same. You can't have one pat answer, for even the same question—or one pat response to *that* response you're *expecting*. That's planning ahead, anticipating what someone will say. Though it's very tempting, "pre-packaged" dialogue doesn't fly. Unless you're reading from an agreed upon, prewritten script, or you happen to be psychic, chances are you can count on something being said that you hadn't figured on.

I'm convinced Marla cooked up her house-tour remarks before showing the place, banking on the fact that her client would throw back completely different responses than those she so disappointedly heard.

Lesson number two is to get accustomed to waiting until you get there (with the dialogue, that is) allowing the conversation to unfold naturally. That doesn't mean you don't prepare for that meeting or presentation—or that you trash-can your agenda or prepared remarks. No, you need to be fully prepared for any situation; that goes without saying. Rather, you just shouldn't be clutching tightly to how you think the conversation *will* or *should* go. For example, when Weatherford gave his first "uh-huh," Marla could have taken that signal as a neon indicator that she should toss aside her well-thought-out script and let the verbal chips fall where they may. But, because she had projected ahead what she thought that conversation would be like, she wound up not only at a loss for words, but disheartened. Expectations are hard to release, but soon you will learn to minimize them— exchange them for an acceptance of what may be. You'll be more receptive to however the dialogue goes and discover how to make the very best of it at that time and place.

WATCHING YOUR STEP

I guess when you break it all down, for most of us, the compulsion to plan or think ahead is merely a means to employ some type of communication safety device. The irony here is that the safer route is to *not* preplan, but to simply go with what *is*. So don't presuppose conversations. In the real world of conversations—there will always be something to contend with other than what you had anticipated. This is an absolute. So as much as you think you have the perfect answer for each and every remark that *could* come up or think you know the direction the conversation will take, forget about it! It's probably not going to happen that way at all, *ever*. Think of it like a ride on the rapids. Though you're geared up and fully prepared to have things go down the way you think they will, the banter, like the rapids, may have you bouncing all over the place. The unexpected waves and currents are what are actually in control (if you've ever negotiated such a ride); the trick is learning how to watch your step and maneuver in and around them. So the next time you get into a conversational canoe, let go of the need to control it and instead embrace the concept that you are ready to go with the flow and are fully willing to expect the unexpected.

I recall once when someone asked me to join him on a river rafting trip. I was horrified just thinking about how risky it would be. I never intended to go on that trip since my idea of camping out is the Beverly Hilton, but just laying awake at night silently anticipating the horror of going on such an adventure is probably akin to what many others experience the night before their important speech (especially the ones with a Q&A segment) or that all-important client meeting. We freak out at the mere prospect of such an "adventure." So, we try to come up with responses to stay in control. Let control go for there is no such thing in real-life conversation.

That's hard, I know.

Consider that the reason you cannot think fast on your feet is because you're constantly planting your feet firmly in what you had pre-conceived—what you imagined you would encounter during that upcoming verbal exchange. This need to "over prepare" is all about perceived safety, but unfortunately, being overly cautious and protective can do just the opposite. It can offer up clear and present danger and hinder spontaneous and appropriate responses.

TIPPING OVER

Something else happens by having a planned script; you wind up throwing yourself off-balance. There you are ready to do "your lines," expecting the other person or persons to do theirs. But when the conversation doesn't unfold the way you thought it would, you find yourself silently renegotiating the script in your head against the actual script—the dialogue that's unfolding in *real time*.

Your canned script could be something you've performed before, so perhaps you're trying to remember that familiar dialogue and rearrange it, to fit the existing conversation. But here's what's happening the whole time you're doing that: You start mentally zigzagging. You're far too busy maneuvering around old stuff or making choices amidst preplanned stuff. In the end, all this causes you to lose time. Downtime means you're slower on the verbal draw. It's like wanting to drive a car in a straight line hurriedly but having to maneuver around those orange cones to get to your destination. When you become bogged down with two or more thoughts, many of which are going in opposite directions at once, how can you get anywhere verbally? You can't, at least not quickly. You often spin. Sometimes you're stuck in the middle of a mental intersection either circling or you're stalled trying to decide which direction to go. This is why so many conversations culminate in a verbal cul de sac and you wind up going nowhere, saying nothing.

Many of my students tell me that being spontaneous is the very quality they lack. As a result, they can feel like it's hours before they can utter a response, and often the one they finally give, they report, is not at all appropriate to the dialogue at hand.

My goal for you is to learn to *be* and *stay* spontaneous in every conversation. Hard to do? Yes, but you're about to learn to let go, stay loose and become far more impromptu than you have ever been before.

WALKING A STRAIGHT LINE

I'm certain you'll agree that, more often than not, when you think an impending conversation *really* counts, you make yourself crazy writing and rewriting "potential" conversations (that often never occur) just to be on the safe side. As a result, spontaneity can't even be a consideration.

Sometimes running possibilities around in your head is an honest part of the preparation process—just good rehearsal for what *may* happen; indeed there is some merit to that and I'll cover that in Chapter Seven. More often than not, though, this process can be harmful rather than helpful. Better to be prepared to answer any questions or comments by knowing your product or material inside and out. You may be safe with a planned opening line, if you're the first to speak, but that's about it. It's freewheeling from there with most conversations.

The whole point of this book and its message is this: **Life for the most part is strictly improvisational, especially when it comes to conversations. So you must learn to free up your mind, let go of any presuppositions, and go with the flow.** It's tempting not to I know. I've worked up "scripts" many a time, for those highly pressurized situations I know are just around the corner. I make a number of assumptions of not only what I anticipate I will say, but I also anticipate what others will say in response to what it is I'm assuming I will say! I can run the entire "what-if" gamut as well as take inventory of my emotional state and the range of feelings I'm experiencing, in a relatively short period of time. But what's the point? Often what I *think* may transpire in a conversation never does—that includes the conversations I dread, like confrontations, important client meetings and (the worst one of all!) being put on the spot unexpectedly. When I begin to anticipate, I have to remind myself to adhere to the Fast Principles (those precepts you're about to learn)!

Maybe this is true for you just like it is for many of my students: The more important the event, the greater the anticipation, thus the more you preplan. On the other hand, when there's little at stake or you're going to be among friendly colleagues, you probably never "run your stuff" ahead of time. In fact, in those cases most people typically say the right thing at the right time no matter what unexpected turns the dialogue takes.

MY SHOES

To make my point, I've recreated an example of what I'm talking about, in terms of anticipating a potential meeting, and what I had presumed might be a difficult conversation, one I was to have with a possible new ExecuProv client.

I frequently meet with would-be clients to discuss how to customize a workshop just for them and what such an event might cost. In this particular instance, I was concerned that this client would challenge me on my workshop fees since I had learned his company was undergoing some downsizing and budget cuts. So, as I prepared for this meeting, I innocently and temporarily slipped out of my Fast On Your Feet posture and began gearing up for what I thought might be the inevitable: A confrontation over what I charge. The following is how I imagined the dialogue would go when we reached the point in the conversation where he would inquire about my fee structure.

HIM:
(Pleasant, but businesslike)
So then, what are your fees?

ME:
(Ready to defend myself)

It depends. In your case—for what you've asked of us—I'll have to consider that I'll be teaching for eight hours and covering three different subjects.

HIM:
(A little tense)

But our budget only calls for a specified amount for each session.

ME:
(Following suit in the tension department)

Yes, of course, I realize that. But I'll need to cover not only my teaching time, but my costs for teachers, travel time, handouts, preparation—you see, my out-of-pocket expenses alone are going to be fairly substantial.

HIM:
(Pressing me)

Well, how much then?

ME:
(Trying to keep my nonchalant composure)

Well, again, it depends. I could cover the public speaking portion and a certain amount of time on speech content, but if we're going to include the dos and don'ts of PowerPoint, then I will need to factor that in. Perhaps we can save the PowerPoint training for another time—or, I know, we could ...

And so it went. In my head, that is. For days. I contemplated his responses versus mine. I had a mental tennis match going on. All in preparation for an event that never transpired the way I thought it would. In fact, every imaginary conversation I ran through my internal thought-processor wasn't even close.

There I was just as ready for my client as Dirty Harry was with his predator. In this particular instance, I had passed my line of rationale by the time I reached the meeting and was in a state of total defensiveness. Go ahead, I thought, *make my day!* Just try and challenge me on my fees. I dare ya! Well, this guy never even challenged my fees. Instead this is how our dialogue actually turned out when we broached the subject of money.

HIM:
(Upbeat and pleasant)

So what are your fees?

ME:
(Following suit, but guarded)

It depends. In your case—for what you've asked for—I'll have to consider that I'll be teaching for eight hours and covering three difference subjects.

HIM:
(Even more pleasant)

Well, I understand your company achieves excellent results so we're willing to pay whatever your daily rates are. Just let purchasing know. Now, how about available dates?

ME
(My mind slipped into bubble bath mode as I heard those words. I was soaking in relief when …)

HIM
(Really corporate-casual)

How does the second week in March look for you and your team?

ME
**(Seemed like forever before I could speak. I hadn't
expected that.)**

Fine. March is … just fine.

I think I missed some of what followed in part of the conversation because my mind was dancing in the streets. All I could hear was Kool and the Gang singing "Celebrate." I exhaled deeply (but quietly) as he showed me his sales team roster. And so it went. It was great. All that preplanning—all that "projected" conversation—all that fretting for nothing!

STEPPING BACK

After that meeting, I asked myself why I didn't just organize my information—do my preparation, get ready, and then *let* go. Why couldn't I have just been willing to expect the unexpected? Why couldn't I have simply been okay with the idea of going with the flow of the conversation, whichever way it went? If he couldn't pay my fee, I could choose to walk away. Or, I could have decided ahead of time how much negotiation room I was willing to allow and leave it at that. I revisited my Fast "playbook" to review the precepts once again. I did a little self-exploration as to why I couldn't *stop* writing that incessant script—all those versions of what I *presumed* the dialogue *might have been* during that meeting. The answer to that question might be the same for you as it was for me: I felt I was responsible for getting a particular result. I felt, if I didn't plan for every eventuality, I might not be able to produce. I often feel I have to be *pre*-pared—handle everything long before it happens, just in case. Once again, even I had to go back to the basics for a quick reminder of the Fast On Your Feet lessons (the same lessons I plan to share with you in this book).

Most of the executives I coach say that anticipating the *unexpected* has become "business as usual" for them. For many, going through the pre-emptive mental drill becomes habit. Habits are hard to break. It's very difficult for most of us *not* to anticipate and play "head games" with ourselves because we're afraid we'll be caught off guard. Once off guard, we won't say the right thing or even anything at all. And if that happens, we may lose the sale, blow an opportunity and/or displease a client or boss. So, we plan and we re-plan. Consequently, we put ourselves through "what-if" conversation-hell.

DIFFERENT STEPS

Even if you have similar situations that occur from day to day, don't forget that people and circumstances always change. What may be appropriate dialogue in one instance, won't be in another. For example, you may have a day planned where you make four identical sales calls, the people you're meeting with hold the same company title, and you're selling the same product or service to each one of them; don't think the conversations will be somewhat identical. Much to the contrary. To make that point, some time later I had another meeting similar to the one I illustrated above (once again we were discussing fees). Surprisingly the agenda took an abrupt turn. Just as my client started discussing money he switched and launched into a discussion of how his company had been duped into a communication skills workshop series that produced less than desirable results. I had no idea that would happen. Suddenly I found myself jumping quickly from one mental place to another. Without skipping a beat, I explained to him how ExecuProv measured its results, and the basics of our 100% guarantee policy. I went with the flow. I had to because life is like that: improvisational and unexpected.

NO KICKING BACK

So that I don't mislead you, let me clarify something. Just because I choose to go with the conversational flow, doesn't mean I just show up and shoot the business-breeze and let the dialogue wander aimlessly. I'll wedge pertinent information into the conversation—but only at the right time. Great improv performers do this consistently as they perform. They have their audience assignment in mind at all times and, if not at first, eventually they find a way to incorporate pre-requested material into a scene. The trick is that they never get anxious about how and when it will happen. They find ways to inject their points, but they never force them or think or plan ahead. We shouldn't either. We should just let the conversation flow. We should just do our improvisational best. We can certainly remain cognizant of strategic opportunities to cover ground we wish to cover. I believe we can keep the "scene" on track and also allow it to unfold without desperately trying to control it. Yes, we can do both at the same time.

It's best to let the conversation *lead you* into what is appropriate dialogue for that moment. If I'm selling my idea, opinion, service, I want to do so in a way that connects and resonates with my audience. That requires me to wait until we get *there*. Not to decide all that ahead of time. So please **be prepared, but don't pre-plan.** There is a big difference between the two.

For homework starters, write down a business situation (or personal one if you wish) that you had today or recently—one in which you found yourself preplanning potential dialogue. First list the situation, next jot down the name of the person (s) in the scene and then recreate what it is you thought would be said. Finally, provide an abbreviated version of how the conversation actually turned out.

SITUATION

_____

_____

_____

THE PERSON (S)

_____

_____

_____

WHAT YOU ANTICIPATED WOULD BE SAID

_____

_____

_____

WHAT WAS ACTUALLY SAID

_____

_____

_____

Take a good look at what you thought would be said versus the outcome. Amazing isn't it? Feel free to repeat this assignment several times, if you wish. This will serve to bring home the point I've been making all along in this chapter; that your actual scene was probably not at all how you *presupposed* it would be. Even if the difference was only slight, note it. It will help to reinforce the theory that conversations never go quite the way we expect.

SURE-FOOTED

Your next assignment is to start readjusting your thinking. I want you to approach each scene—each piece of dialogue for one whole day (though I'm certain you'll want to do it even after one day!) with the same mindset as that of improv comedy players. Remember, one of their secrets is that they venture into verbal territory with blind faith. This is the very first fundamental principle each improv comedy player learns. They trust that they will say the right thing at the right time, *every* time, and they also demonstrate trust to those with whom they find themselves in scenes. They also firmly trust the process, knowing that everything *will* work out on stage for them if they let go of anticipating or forcing a scene to go a certain way. They relinquish control. They forego the urge to force any specific idea or action into play. Instead they stay in the moment.

Here's another key: It's what improv players term: "Be here now." They never lag behind the conversation (thinking about what they could or should have said), nor do they jump ahead, anticipating where the dialogue is headed or should go. Improv players learn that no matter what is said, they will stay current and present at all times.

Through the repetitiveness of staying present and holding true to the notion of complete trust, improv comedy players project a confident and positive posture as they enter any improv scene. Why? Because they've already accepted—and I mean fully accepted—that they have no control over how that scene will unfold. They are trained to be comfortable dealing with the unpredictable and the unknown. They fully comprehend that they can only control themselves and not the other player (s). They also come to learn that by adhering to these beginning improv concepts, of letting go and staying in the moment, they will undoubtedly come upon the right and appropriate responses every time because they're tightly weaving one piece of dialogue to the next. This foundational mindset takes time to nurture and build, of course. But, these ideas, of relinquishing control, staying in the present, and trusting in self, are failsafe precepts to making unexpected communication with others work. Always. You can do the same. And like any other mental discipline, this mindset takes time to develop and master.

Improv comedy performers build on one success after another and eventually become desensitized to the fear of not being able to say something, fast. After they have accumulated enough victories dealing with the unexpected, they learn that somehow, someway, a scene will just take care of itself.

Throughout the book I'm asking you to function like the improv comedy player! Don't worry though you'll be doing the instruction one step at a time. I plan to teach you some improv comedy "rules and tools" as we go along and once you've become acquainted with them, the rest will be easy.

HOP, SKIP AND A JUMP

As I mentioned earlier, improv comedy players tell me performing in an improv comedy scene is like mental bungee jumping. After enough experiences doing it, they come to know they won't splatter against the verbal mountainside. Instead, they swing freely, going with each movement (spoken line) and allowing that experience to *take them* in whatever direction it goes.

They are totally spontaneous! Now that's not to suggest that they enter a scene with no regard for the "set up"—that is, the request from the audience of who they are, what they're doing and particulars the audience has asked of them, such as working out a specific conflict or problem. As I mentioned before, all that is kept in mind. But they maneuver around those particulars, stay with the conversation as it unfolds in the moment, and simply let that scene happen, line by line! Through it all they focus on staying spontaneous.

Spontaneity is at the heart of the improv player's performance strategy and I want it to be at the heart of yours, too.

After accepting the idea that they don't *have* control, they realize they don't *need* to control a scene to make it work. The same holds true for you and me! The key? Improv players' minds are far more relaxed and loose, which enables them to go with the flow—quickly and comfortably. It's hard to be mentally nimble when you're mind is rigid; when it is anticipating something specific and holding fast to *that* outcome.

Think of improv comedy players like great athletes who train endlessly to get strong and fit to compete. When it comes time to "perform," the athletes have done so many workouts in preparation that their physical muscles respond with "muscle memory." Improv players are like that with their mental muscles. Once it is trained, the mind does not forget!

I'm asking you to think and behave like an improv comedy player. I want you to start by latching onto these basic Fast On Your Feet principles:

- Learn to trust yourself and others
- Promise you will stay in the moment—"be here now"
- Be more willing to relinquish control
- Decide to let go and allow yourself to be more spontaneous.

MARCHING ONWARD

Since the core lesson in this chapter is all about expecting the unexpected, I've set forth a few homework assignments that will help you develop greater self-trust, relinquish control, be more adventuresome and spontaneous, and be more relaxed in an arena that is probably not your comfort zone. Some assignments may seem silly, but each is designed to help you become more carefree as you learn to expect and deal with the unexpected.

1. **Go grocery shopping.** Don't buy any of the same brands or products you usually buy. If you buy ice cream, try frozen yogurt. If it's always broccoli, choose Brussels sprouts. Stuck on salmon? Pick trout. Or, change categories all together. Instead of ice cream, buy cookies and so on. Be spontaneous about this grocery excursion. I became so routine with my grocery shopping, that I could have blindfolded myself and still stocked up! But one week, I actually forced myself to do something different—to treat my taste buds to the unexpected. I told myself I wouldn't buy any identical grocery item that I had purchased before. I had a blast! (Okay, so I hated the fat-free Lay's.) But, every time I opened the pantry and the fridge, I surprised myself. It was one unexpected experience after another. I, like so many others I know, get into eating ruts. But this exercise taught me a lot. I learned to adapt and adjust quickly to food items I didn't generally buy. It made me more open, more willing, and gave me an overall feeling of not needing to control things as simple as my daily food intake. Now I want you to try this. It's fun! It will force you out of stagnant habit patterns and make you more aware of what you're doing in the *present*. It takes more immediate focus to scan the other brands instead of just picking up the same old box of rice, for instance. It also takes trust and letting go of control to be spontaneous enough to try foods you never before considered.

2. **Ask your spouse or one of your children to pick out the outfit you'll wear to work tomorrow without showing it to you.** Instruct him or her to choose a clothing ensemble that's appropriate, of course, but a combination you wouldn't ordinarily put together yourself. When you get up in the morning and dress for work, you will be

dealing with the unexpected! Go with the flow. Don't question his or her choices, just suit up! Since this is very personal, it's a good exercise. It makes you realize how formulated, structured, "pre-packaged" and controlling you really are!

3. **Make an effort to have a conversation with someone at the office you normally don't interact with.** Focus on staying in the moment and just let the conversation flow. Notice how much of that conversation turns out to be dialogue you couldn't have anticipated. Also take note of how easy it is to go with the flow when you do so from moment to moment.

4. **If you have the kind of working relationship that will allow for it, ask your boss or fellow colleagues to throw an assignment at you—one that you weren't expecting, at a time when you least expect it.** One example might be that your boss insists you give a 10-minute speech at the Monday morning staff meeting on the merits of the new budget proposal—something you hadn't anticipated, but know something about. This homework assignment lends itself well to a situation where *you* have to do the talking before others—one where you're put on the spot and have to react appropriately, and of course, instantly. Whatever it is, let your boss know it has to be something that you are familiar with, but an assignment that will challenge the way you deal with the subject matter.

5. **Have a friend take you to a movie you wouldn't normally see, or a restaurant you never frequent; and tell them not to let you know where it is they're taking you.** Revel in your ability to adapt to the unfamiliar and enjoy every moment of it!

6. **Get a group together and play charades, Pictionary, Password, improv games** …Make it some fun activity that challenges your sense of teamwork, stimulates mental agility, and deals with the unexpected.

7. **As a drill, rehearse — during conversations with customers and co-workers during meetings, sales calls**

and other work related situations. Engage in dialogue that is not preplanned in any way. Try not to anticipate what will be said and try not to control the direction in which the scene is headed. Trust that you can be spontaneous and simply let the scene lead you. This exercise is one I would like you to do at least once a day, if not more!

If you can think of similar assignments that promote the willingness to expect the unexpected and let go, then do them. Using your creativity and setting yourself up for surprises are all part of the Fast On Your Feet process. The more you stretch and tone your mental muscles, the easier it will be for you to loosen up, become nimble and quick, and ultimately confident. Just like any other skilled improv player, you'll eventually become unfazed by the uncertainty of any communication situation. With enough practice, your work will result in new habits—positive ones. These habits will build on one another. Soon you will have the mental alacrity, the trust and the confidence to consistently summon up whatever it is you want or need to say when ….

Now let's move forward for a discussion on the pair that pinch—two very specific reasons why it is, often times, we *cannot* be fast on our feet.

"These are just killing me ..."

Chapter Two

THE PAIR THAT PINCH:
Two Reasons Why You Can't Be Fast On Your Feet

<u>**WHO SWIPED THE PROTOTYPE? –TAKE ONE**</u>

INT. R&D BOSS' OFFICE. BIG DEAL TECHNOLOGY. MID-AFTERNOON

Close up: Joan, terrified. Blood flow surging from limbs to trunk of body. In defense, crosses legs, folds arms tightly, tucks them close to her chest. Hunches over for warmth. Chin tilts downward. Tries to avoid eye contact with Cavendish who's challenging the R&D team again on its performance. Joan hopes he doesn't key in on her. Camera pulls back for wide shot to include others around the table.

CANVENDISH
(Pins his stare on Joan)

Joan, let me rephrase the question.

(An octave higher. More demand than query)

Why is it we don't have the prototype?!!!

JOAN

I ... I ... you see ... I ...

CAVENDISH
(In his worst Regis)

Is that your final answer?

JOAN

No, well, I mean ...

CAVENDISH
(Annoyance escalating)

You mean what?

JOAN
(Thoughts race through her head. Wants desperately to
provide complicated yet viable explanation. Sits frozen.
Stares at floor. Finally ... shrugs)

CUT

WHO CAN MOVE FAST IN THIS PAIR?

When I begin the exploration process with each one of my
students to determine why it is that they *can't* be fast on their
feet, it always comes down to one or both of two specific reasons:
Fear and inhibition. It never fails. These two culprits pinch our
mental muscles—actually cut off the natural flow of thinking and
ease of thought-to-speech. They halt reasonable and appropriate
responses, as well as those that could be clever, humorous and
even brilliant.

Fear and/or inhibition can be induced by inner or outer stimuli.

As you can see, Joan's inability to respond to Cavindish was initially induced by fear—fear of him challenging her. However, when I met with her sometime after this incident she was carrying her "Canvendish phobia" (and her slumped body posture) into similar meetings and situations with other superiors. She was wearing fear and inhibition like a pair of painfully narrow and worn-down pumps. She told me that it was hard for her to navigate many of her business communications for she had taken to calling up the Cavendish experience that had started it all (outer stimuli) and it had now become a source of her constant trepidation (inner stimuli). As her fear began to escalate, she simply kept shutting down. By the time she reached me, she stated she was rendered nearly speechless in every meeting situation. I sincerely felt sorry for her. Getting to that point would be a demoralizing experience for any of us!

I'll tell you what I tell all my students and what I explained to Joan: Getting to and understanding the cause of why you can't be fast on your feet is the first step in conquering the problem. It's very individual and personal. So, I assured Joan, by recognizing that Cavendish was at the heart of her problem, she was well on her way to getting beyond her fear and inhibition. After understanding comes acceptance, I told her, and acceptance is followed by some type of positive action.

I offered Joan the same Fast techniques I offer those I coach every day. And now it's time to offer them to you. It begins with identifying what it is that makes you fearful and what it is that causes you to withdraw.

FEET FIRST

I want to hone in on a bit more about the pair that "pinches" and point out some of the most common root causes for butting up against fear and inhibition as we go about our everyday business life.

There's no debate that fear and inhibition can stop any of us dead in our tracks and preclude us from being able to respond readily. By the way, for many business professionals, it doesn't take much of either one for that to happen! Mainly it's because some of us are frightened that they we will say or do something foolish, while some of us are fearful we will be exposed. So in either case we become so frightened and shut down—so panicky or repressed—that we are unable to go with our innate and (very often) appropriate impulses. This is what happened to Joan even though she had justification for the R&D shortfall: The vendor had not delivered the materials in time for the team to assemble the prototype on schedule.

Since Cavindish had heard this (real) excuse a month earlier, she told me, it was obvious to Joan he wasn't going to buy it a second time. No matter how much it was not her fault or the fault of the others on the R&D team, Cavendish still had a tendency to blame the outcome on his employees, primarily Joan. When Cavendish's focus went to Joan that day she was reluctant to offer any excuse like she had previously. The situation was further exacerbated when Cavendish approached her in an accusatory way. As you could see, it left her stymied—just stupefied. So she sat there saying nothing. Truly, she didn't want to be dressed down in front of the others. And, she told me, she hated feeling so vulnerable!

RUNNING SCARED

Some people, in a given business situation or circumstance, fear themselves, while others initially fear those individuals or the circumstances around them (like Joan). Sometimes the fear is generated from both sources (inner and outer) simultaneously. It could be that you feel ill-prepared or unknowledgeable and as your mind churns and even obsesses over the stress of being put on the spot, you become afraid of going into a situation that may prompt you to say something ridiculous or downright stupid. This is why you often say nothing. That's the inner factor.

Then there are outer reasons. See if any of these sound familiar: Perhaps the boss just interrupted you in order to correct you in front of everyone or someone in the meeting or audience threw a deprecating look your way. Maybe the fear arises out of the stark reality that a huge contract could be hanging on your very pitch, or a promotion is at stake; the one you've been hoping for for months. Other common situations often include the all-important job interview. Or how about this one: The team you're responsible for leading may have sent off signals in the middle of a critical meeting that left you feeling overwhelmed, like they intimated they should be leading *you*.

Reluctance to open your mouth and respond quickly and spontaneously might also be due to a bundle of fears, not just one in particular.

In one situation, I had a client who was up for reappointment to a very important post on the panel of a governmental agency—an assignment she had held for six years. When it was time for the board review, she sat facing five people who were all firing questions at her (she didn't know ahead of time what those queries might be). She had never met two of the interviewers before. She was also keenly aware that one of those asking questions had close political ties to an individual who followed her in the interview process; a guy who wanted her job. What horrified her even more, she confided, was that she was an attorney and since many of the questions were technical in nature regarding environmental pollution issues, she was concerned she would not be free to provide satisfactory answers. She was also well aware that if she stalled or hedged on any one of the questions, her fear would give her away and/or the panel would decide/determine she was unknowledgeable and in over her head.

As you can see, this woman was dealing with terror on many fronts both internally and externally. It was her nature to clam up when under fire and just freeze, but after several coaching sessions (seven hours total), and after arming her with a bag of Fast tricks, she approached this meeting with a different mindset and one that proved beneficial. Her contract was renewed.

TIP-TOEING THROUGH THE TWO LIPS

But as with this woman, fear and inhibition seem to take the driver's seat for most business professionals when something important is on the line. And, as I've mentioned, often it is not one thing that scares you in a difficult communications situation, it could be several and they can all gang up and hit simultaneously. It's a lot for the mind to modulate while attempting to appear confident and poised and, *most of all*, respond quickly.

Fear is fear for whatever reason, real or imagined; and no one functions well when fear overtakes them. Without some diligent preparation and without a different mindset, the client I just mentioned could have been buried beneath her trepidation (for she had succumbed to it many times before, I later found out). And during each of those times, she readily confessed, her mind had jammed; she simply sat mute, unable to fire off a response. Like Joan, she was frozen in fear. She told me after she learned of her reappointment that she was sure her brisk and confident responses to the panel's questions are what garnered her a second term. And therein lies what is key: appearing confident by answering or responding readily.

How does someone like Joan mitigate her fears and how do her newly acquired skills apply to you? Keep reading!

I have yet to hold a workshop on the "Fast" topic where even the boldest of senior executives didn't confess that there was some*thing* or some*one* in their work environs that truly did scare them. In a moment, I'll ask you to ponder what pushes your panic button (s), but first, let me round out my discussion by addressing the second culprit that cuts you off at the mental knees and keeps you from being fast on your feet: Inhibition.

STEP INSIDE

Inhibition, like the fear factor, can be caused from internal or external stimuli. We *become* inhibited we don't come into the world that way. That's not to say that some personalities are not more quiet, passive and introverted, certainly they are, but no one is born inhibited, I don't believe. Children are usually very open and forthcoming until some incident or certain circumstance causes them to behave otherwise. So, if you find yourself trying to chalk up your inhibition and your inability to being fast on your feet to heredity, think again, something in your life experience altered your personality along the way.

Just like fear (the other one that pinches off the verbal flow), inhibition can also be caused from a host of reasons. It could be a typical reaction that manifests itself when a person is caught in what they perceive to be an uncomfortable or confrontational situation. For instance, I work with many individuals who function openly and freely among trusted colleagues, friends and family members. They display no inhibitions whatsoever. They are spontaneous and always on top of saying the right thing at the right time. It's only when such individuals are made to feel uncomfortable or pressured in the presence of others that they clam up and are unable to go with their innate instincts and impulses.

Through my work I have discovered that many of us clutch in the face of pressure (like when the boss unexpectedly enters the meeting or does what Cavindish did to Joan), while others find themselves unable to be fast on their feet as a result of some unique situation (they've never liked the sound of their own voice, for instance, or they can't seem to gather the right words when they so desperately need them).

I don't know what inhibits you, but just as we're going to look fear squarely in the eye, we're going to do the same with inhibition. Soon I'll ask you to examine and list what it is that *represses* you, but for now here are a few of the most common complaints I get: Things were fine until the cranky client walked in … my speech was sailing along and then an audience member challenged me on a point I just made in the Q &A portion of my speech … I suddenly realized someone in the room knew more about the subject than I did.

Maybe for you it's the big mouth colleague who randomly spouts something off that makes you shrink inside yourself. Maybe it's because your biggest sale of the year is on the table and you don't want to blow the deal, so you play it close to the vest—approach the situation cautiously, conservatively. Or, could it be that your ex just popped into your presentation (the one no one in the office knew you had been seeing?). Ever make a verbal faux pas, someone laughs and your face turns beet red? Suddenly your happy countenance goes to a sullen repose and you'd like to take the fetal position. Yes, embarrassment is a huge inhibitor. Whatever it is that makes you put a lid on what it was you were *going to say*—embarrassment, humiliation, uncertainty; it doesn't matter. Whatever it is that forces you to retreat is what I want to help you overcome so you will never again choke at those all too important times when you need to say *something* ...

WALKING A FINE LINE

As I suggested earlier, once someone has a negative experience and goes within, when each subsequent like situation occurs, inhibition not only grows—it flourishes. For example, if you've always been one who dislikes standing and addressing a group, whether it's three or 300, each time you're required to do so you can dig a deeper groove into your mental cave of inhibition. Perhaps you're inhibited out of self-consciousness. Maybe it's tied to your physical appearance like thinning hair, an overbite or being overweight. Or could it be something else entirely, like the fact that you never got that college degree that everyone else in the department seems to have, or you're carrying around all that baggage related to the time when you were chastised in front of a group for once saying something inane? I knew a human resources director who would blush (and give himself away) as he wrote down a word he didn't understand during staff meetings (to look it up later). He said his lacking vocabulary was the reason he rarely spoke. He didn't want to draw attention to himself.

I coached another who had never been able to get up the courage to participate in the brainstorming sessions for the quality control meetings because when he was five his father laughed out loud mockingly at his suggestion that the family dress up as pilgrims and Indians at the Thanksgiving table. Even now at 50, he was still terrified of offering an idea that might recreate something reminiscent of that humiliating moment. Inhibitions are powerful; they can cause such deep and aggravated repression that you may never be able to emerge from your shell even under the most non-threatening communication circumstances. So you can only imagine what happens to the inhibited as a result of those tense "fast on your feet" moments.

Inhibition and fear can put the brakes on any motor skills including thought, speech and movement. Interesting how one feeds off another. Certainly such was the case with Joan and the other gal I mentioned. When we're afraid, we become inhibited.

And, feeling repressed, can spark fear—a panic that we won't be able to produce, verbally. The two are so closely linked and reactive to each other.

AN IMPORTANT STEP

As you come to understand how antithetical fear and inhibition are to the ability to be quick and nimble, you've taken an important step (pardon the pun) in tackling the problem.

Examine then how powerful both fear and inhibition are and what part they play in shutting down your mental processes. Next, take a cursory look at how these two dynamics have affected, thus far, those business "scenes" in your professional life; those times when you desperately needed to be fast on your feet, but couldn't produce.

Before working with them, many of my students had simply resigned themselves to the belief that they would have to carry around their fears and inhibitions for the remainder of their professional lives. They claimed there was no way out and the best they could do was to struggle through their strained communication moments, hoping at least for a few wins along the way. I say, rubbish! No one has to settle for that existence and concede that that's just the way it's been and will always be. Quite the contrary: We should come to expect very few defeats.

Know this: Even if you have established a pattern whereby you have allowed fear and inhibition to overrun your extemporaneous responses, you can reverse this habit. There is no reason why you, like those I have personally coached, can't change this dynamic. It just takes time, skill and practice, and new information.

STICKING A TOE IN THE WATER

If you've allowed the pair that pinches to dominate your psyche, you can change all that by first identifying what it is that happens to you, and why, when you're put on the spot; when you can't seem to offer an appropriate comeback.

To begin, I would like to suggest you latch on to a new resolve: You *will* learn the techniques that will assure your success in handling every communication situation (unexpected, confrontational, adversarial or uncomfortable) with rapid and appropriate responses. Mustering the determination to lick this problem is one of the most important steps you can take as you set the stage to learn new skills; techniques that are geared to mitigate fear and unleash inhibitions.

With that in mind, I would like to ask you now to make the identification process by listing your communication fears. Include what it is that suddenly sends you into a stage of fright during those times when you're required to be fast on your feet, but just can't seem to be. To get you thinking, here are a few examples of what I'm talking about:

- My boss suddenly walks into the staff meeting and asks me to explain the technicalities of the competitive analysis; a report I've never really understood
- One of my subordinates puts a question to me about pay raises
- Out of the blue my client challenges his billing statement
- I'm called on at the breakfast meeting without notice to talk about a topic I know little about
- I want to gracefully bow out of heading up the company picnic
- A business colleague starts flirting with me
- I'm asked to introduce the guest speaker and I was so busy I forgot I had to do this; consequently I left my notes at home

Now make your list. It can be general in terms of types of scenarios—a broad overview—but make certain you list instances where you were genuinely scared out of your wits. You can also list those situations that haven't happened to you yet, but you dread they might. One example could be thoughts of being asked to give an impromptu toast at your boss' retirement dinner. Don't let the number of entries on this worksheet limit you. Write down as many as you wish. The objective is for you to clearly identify business circumstances and situations that cause sheer panic.

1. _____
2. _____

3. _____
4. _____
5. _____

Next, it's time to take at look at your inhibitions—what root causes seem to impede your natural verbal flow. Here are a few examples I've saved from my students:

- If the majority of those in the meeting are the other gender, I tend to sink into my chair
- I need to be formal and reserved in order to be appropriate and taken seriously in business situations
- I tend to stammer when I'm nervous. Being called upon impromptu always makes my chin quiver which embarrasses me
- I'm 30 pounds overweight and everyone in my department has the body of Jennifer Aniston, so I sit in the corner so as not to be noticed
- Most of the people in my field have MBAs; I have only a BA
- The time I was unexpectedly asked to give a humorous account of what my boss looked like rolling down the stairwell, I bombed

Now it's time for your list. Once again, don't limit yourself to a few. You can scribble down everything including inhibitions you've brought from childhood (my mother told me if I couldn't say anything nice not to say it at all, for instance, so often that precludes me for sticking up for myself) to recent situations that caused you to dampen your intrinsic responses.

1. _____
2. _____
3. _____
4. _____
5. _____

NOTHIN' GONNA BREAK YOUR STRIDE

Congratulations! You've made huge strides by having identified what you're afraid of and what inhibits you. I always tell my ExecuProv charges that when they can identify and face their fears and pinpoint what hinders them, their work as improv students is well on its way. I tell my improv comedy students there is no way they can master that art form if they allow fear or inhibition to creep into their heads during an onstage moment. So as you can imagine, they spend weeks working out, doing drills, and building confidence in order to replace any reluctance they may have had toward blurting out dialogue quickly and spontaneously. You, too, can gain the same fearless and uninhibited posture.

Another note on grappling with the pair that pinch: Realize that when we are enslaved by fear and inhibition, we are also easily intimidated. We can feel threatened by person, place or thing! I have discovered that many of my students, on a daily basis, feel intimidated by clients, superiors and colleagues (like Joan). When you release your inhibitions and square off with your fears, and master many of the same basics as that of the improv comedy actor, you can't possibly be intimidated by anything or anyone, most notably in the context of a business setting. So if the boss or your biggest client walks in and unexpectedly puts you on the hot seat, with your new skills in tow, you'll meet that challenge quickly, confidently and with a big smile.

Sound good? All this talk about the pair that pinches makes sense? But, you may be asking, how do I get rid of my fears and how can I free my inhibitions? Well, that's the lesson in the subsequent chapter: Finding the antidote to those two nuisances, for like a pair of shoes that are just too tight or fit poorly, fear and inhibition truly can cramp your style. That's the last thing I want to have happen to you!

Before moving forward, where you will learn what the improvisational comedy player learns, I want to assign a few homework tasks to help you face your fears and lessen your inhibitions:

FEAR

1. **Do at least one activity that has always frightened you and that you have completely avoided.** This could be something physical like skiing, taking a dip in the deep

end of the pool, riding a roller coaster, or it could be something else entirely. For me it would be baking a cake or learning to fly a plane (the world would be a much safer place if I did the latter). For you it might be sitting in a dark room with no light on for 10 minutes. Please don't do anything where you could hurt yourself (!) but something that you've always said, *No, I can't possibly do that … it terrifies me!* This is the time to stretch and to realize that there are things you no longer need to fear. Here's one: how about putting some humor into that next speech?

2. **Confront a person that has been irritating you and discuss (nicely) your grievance.** For me it would be my bank manager. I hate those lines that take forever, but I've always been afraid if I complained to him he would accidentally misplace my money.

3. **If you've shied away from trying a new hobby** like writing poetry, write a poem. If you sing quietly in the church choir, ask to perform a solo.

Continue this preliminary assignment by adding activities to this list (at least three more—half a dozen in all). Be courageous and by all means reward yourself for a job well done each time you march boldly forward and tackle a new challenge. My reward? A piece of Gharadelli dark chocolate!

INHIBITION

Naturally, I'm going to ask you to do a few prerequisite tasks to get you to loosen up. As I instructed in the section above, I want you to do things you wouldn't ordinarily do because you've just been too "up tight" to try them. Remember the student who wanted to dress like a pilgrim at the Thanksgiving table? I urged him to host a Halloween party and dress like he'd just stepped off the Mayflower. He did and reported that it had done wonders in terms of freeing him from the shackles within. He still wears that hat with the buckle in the front!

I will now offer a few just to get you thinking:

1. **Join a community theater and sign on to do a play,** even a cameo role in a show will do. You won't believe how wonderful it will be when you take the stage and deliver those lines! This is something I'm sure you never even considered, but I truly believe it's a great way to open the door and shoo inhibition away.

2. **If you don't typically dance, go dancing.** Take to the dance floor and really let loose. Make up your own dance style. Act confident as you do. Soon people will begin to follow your groove, for with that attitude on your face and in your body language, they will think they need to learn that new dance of yours or be left out in the cold. If you dance already, find another similar activity that will force you to be on "display." Do this with no shame. In fact put a big smile on your face. I knew a swing dancer who took up ballet. He was 6'3" and weighed 240 pounds. He claims it was one of the most liberating experiences of his life!

3. **If you're female and concerned about maintaining an impeccable appearance, go out without makeup on,** even if it's to the grocery store. You'll be surprised how doing something like this helps you shed unwanted inhibitions. If you're a guy, do something silly like get a sign that says "Will Stand On Street Corner With Sign To Alleviate Inhibitions" and take to the streets with it. Who knows, maybe you'll make a few bucks!

For those of you who need to lessen your inhibitions in baby steps, tap into what makes you feel inhibited and find a way to reverse that inhibition. For example, if you've been too afraid to show your temper, go outside and thrust a mud clod against the fence. It'll make you feel good, and oh so loose!

Just as I requested in the previous assignment regarding overcoming fear, make sure you do at least half a dozen tasks that promote freeing you up internally and ones that you will find satisfying.

Now that your feet are off the ground, in terms of priming yourself to becoming braver and more willing, let's move forward and begin your work at mental boot camp. This is the improvisational comedy actor's training ground; the one that holds all the secrets you're about to acquire. The secrets that will surely make you fast on your feet!

Chapter Three

FANCY FOOTWORK:
Preparing for When You're Least Prepared

<u>**LUNCH IS ON ME – TAKE ONE**</u>

INT. MARRIOTT HOTEL BANQUET MEETING ROOM – MONTHLY WOMEN'S ALLIANCE BUSINESS LUNCHEON MEETING

FADE IN:

Camera zooms past back of women's heads seated at circular, linen-covered lunch tables. Closes in on woman standing before lectern. Petite brunette nervously shifts to next 3x5 card

RACHEL
(Pleasant and upbeat)

... she's also very talented as an interior decorator, although she's here today to speak to you about the how-to's of starting your own business, **(laughs nervously attempting one-liner)** not how to Feng-shui your office.

Joke well-received. Laughs all around

RACHEL
(Deep sigh. Continues)

I am proud to welcome Becky Mandel to the Women's Alliance business luncheon meeting today because she is one of the few ...

RACHEL
(Catches glimpse of association's president, Millie Armstrong, rear of room, standing, waving arms wildly. Resembles technician on tarmac signaling *don't land here.*)

MILLIE
(Mouthing words)

She's not here yet.

RACHEL
(Registering the shock. Eyes shoot back terror. Rehearsed all morning for three minute intro. All she could do to muster intro. Now what?)

Uh ...um ...

MILLIE
(Fingers look like she's pulling imaginary taffy. Stretch it sign)

RACHEL

(Eyes widen)

MILLIE
(Hands extend wider. Dips knees for more emphasis on *keep going*)

RACHEL
(Does not understand the concept: ad lib)

FREEZE FRAME

It certainly would have behooved Rachel to have taken some improv comedy classes. If she had, she would have kept right on rolling with her narrative, covering the mishap even if she herself had to fill the hour-long slot slated for the noontime speaker. If the speaker hadn't shown up at all, perhaps she could have started a discussion among the attendees asking how each of them had started their businesses, what advice they could share, and what assistance they might need to make their businesses more successful. Had she wished to talk about the second subject she mentioned, Feng-shui, she could have taken off on that topic; maybe asking each attendee to tell the rest of the audience what annoyed them about their office décor. She may have followed that by rousting up a lively discussion among the group, getting each of them to share ideas with one another. These ideas could have included everything from how to deal with difficult clients to the selection of invigorating color schemes to spice up the office space. But Rachel, like so many others, was not prepared for the unexpected. She was thrown for a loop!

I have been in a number of situations where I was stuck just like Rachel. I recall one afternoon during an ExecuProv workshop when I was to introduce a company vice president who was to take over the class to educate his subordinates on what he expected in the way of their PowerPoint presentations. Ralph (not his real name, but I don't want to embarrass him) confessed to me at the start of the session that he was very nervous about public speaking and since he knew his boss would be in the audience, he was concerned he would be heavily scrutinized. Apparently, the mere thought kicked off some bodily functions that sent him rushing to the restroom. There I was, having to fake it, not knowing if he would return or not. He had a 40-minute presentation. Yikes! After a short time of ad-libing, I quietly and diplomatically asked if anyone knew where Ralph was. Someone handed me a note. It read: *Ralph's in the bathroom. Says he can't leave.* I made some gracious excuse for him to the audience—told them he was stuck with the head … of purchasing (I think I said) on an emergency conference call. I then jumped in and covered the topic he was about to address. Had it not been for all the times I was on stage acting out impromptu suggestions from the audience, I may have lost it, but I'm used to *covering*.

Have I ever been thrown for a loop? Yes, once. My improv skills were forcibly put to the test at my father's funeral. This is a true story—one that could fit perfectly into a Woody Allen movie. My sister and I had hired a minister to officiate at a graveside service; a simple affair with about three-dozen close friends and family. I was seated in the front row beneath a canopy overhead to shield the unforgiving August sun. I had been my father's chief caregiver, and had also officiated over the last stages of his life. It was finally my turn to have a good cry and I really needed one. I had had to be the strong one through his eight-year battle with Alzheimer's. So there I sat ready to let someone else take the helm so I could spill my grief.

After waiting nearly 25 minutes, it was apparent the minister wasn't going to show. My sister gave me one of those *you better do something looks* and I jumped out of my seat, stifled my tears and approached the jazz singer (a friend) who I had asked to sing at what was to be a fairly short service. I asked her to start *vamping, scatting, humming* …" She suddenly added "Satin Doll" and a jazz rendition of "Amazing Grace" to the play-list that was to only have included one song that day, my dad's favorite tune, "Here's to Life."

When she finished the first two songs, I began to address the audience. I talked about my father's wonderful life as a jazz musician and then I asked those who wished to do so to share a few stories. No one really wanted to share so I continued on. I closed by asking everyone to share in a prayer. Then Karen, the singer, sang the final tune. Now for many of those in attendance, they probably thought that was the way we had planned it. Not at all, but it worked. The affair turned out beautifully.

Well, you may be thinking, easy for her, she's a natural. Not really. I spent years honing my craft, and when I needed to fall back on it, my skill set was solidly in place. It carried me through. You will get to the point where you can do the same.

THE KICK OFF

Many people think that the improvisational comedy actor is born quick, mentally agile, uninhibited and spontaneous, but in most instances that is simply not the case. I, just like the other performers who develop this craft, work diligently at it. Improv comedy players study techniques on how to be swift, nimble and ready. They learn tricks and secrets for how to be prepared when they are least prepared, which is most of the time when they are on stage. Some study for weeks and months while others do so for years (like me). The skill set they acquire is geared to tone and increase the use of the mental muscles. With enough practice, they can easily double or triple the speed with which their minds work. When faced with situations like Rachel's and the incident at my father's funeral (my biggest improv challenge to date), they call up those superb skills to carry them through.

If it can work for me and for Rachel, and for improvisational comedy players across the country, it can work for you.

The work of the improv comedy player is demanding and intense yet the legitimately trained performers who engage in this art form seem to sail easily through the process each and every time. How do they do that? They learn rules and tools and stretch and toughen up their mental muscles with mental aerobics.

What they're up against and how they train for such random demands is of particular importance to you for you are about to learn the same techniques and drills that enable them to think *consistently* fast on their feet. Though I will touch on several of their rules, since they aptly apply to what you will need for your "tool belt," there are a select few that I will emphasize because these are keenly designed to promote mental agility, spontaneity, quick verbal reflexes and self-confidence.

STEP ONE

To begin the Fast On Your Feet process, you must establish

a whole new mindset. I want you to tell yourself, despite how many times you may have faltered when put on the spot in the past, that you *can* learn to come up with the right response at the right time. Okay, that's number one. Number two is paramount and is the answer to changing how you view critical unexpected situations. You must tell yourself, *ah, who cares*. Remember in the bigger picture, none of those moments are a do-or-die situation. So ask yourself, *is **this** really all that important to me*?

I tell all my ExecuProv students to stand back and calculate whether or not the situation in which they feel somehow mentally and verbally trapped truly warrants the importance they give it. Here's how they typically make that assessment. They create two lists: The Number One List itemizes things that *really* count. The Number Two List is a rundown of things that are irrelevant or insignificant in the overall scheme of things. For example, on the first list you might include your health, your family, your friends, your spiritual beliefs and so on, while the second list might include material possessions and, yes, even your job. Most people put far too much emphasis on their professional station in life, in fact, so much so that sadly that is where they find their identity. That can be a dangerous thing for if you lose a job, or a client, or the contract goes to someone else, you may feel as though some of your self-esteem has gone out the door with it!

I also tell both my improv players and my ExecuProv students that when you *care too much* you set yourself up for potential failure and grave disappointment. Caring too much interferes with the ability to say something when you *need* to. Caught up in all that caring, you spend too much time dwelling on what it is you think you *should* or *should not* say rather than allowing your mental processes to flow fluidly so that you can intelligently, and spontaneously, come up with all of the *right* answers.

When I coach actors who are going on auditions, I remind them that it is essential to embody this nonchalant mindset. Casting directors can sense instantly if an actor has any hint of desperation and are turned off by anyone who seems needy, nervous or uncomfortable. Now if an improv player (consider yourself one because you've just crossed the threshold of Improv Boot Camp and are required to do improv all day long in your job) is in this uptight state, he or she will die on stage because success is completely dependent upon the ability to be spontaneous. Improv players who worry about what the audience or the other players will think, or (this is a big one), whether or not *they are funny*—will stifle their mental and verbal rhythms completely. Those who approach each improv assignment with the attitude: a*h who cares*, and implement their skill set every step of the way, are enormously successful at this demanding art form.

My friend, Michael Gellman, who has been a director at Second City in Chicago for many years (one of the country's most renowned improvisational comedy organizations), always asks his actors to recite one of Second City's sacred mantras before they take to the stage: *Screw It*. He tells them to hold fast to this attitude adjustment and then to see the mind as a blank canvas that will fill itself up naturally once they hit the stage. That can only happen, he cautions, if they adopt this a*h, who cares* state of mind. If they worry they will probably choke.

I've gone so far as to tell many of my ExecuProv students to imagine that they've won the lottery. With several million in the bank they really don't need their respective jobs. With that in mind I ask them, *how much do you care now?* They usually give me one of those *I **don't** care after all* shrugs. If business professionals could only acquire this mindset, fear and inhibition would miraculously vanish and they would be far more apt to give rapid and appropriate responses.

KICKING BACK

I mentioned earlier that most people have little fear of communication issues when they are dialoguing with those they feel most comfortable—friends, family, work buddies. But when it's the boss, the big client or that person at work that makes them uncomfortable, they are bound to be subject to brain freeze.

I was concerned it might happen to me. When I first left the improv stage and hit the speaking circuit in Corporate America, I was genuinely terrified (**FEAR**) for this new type of audience seemed so foreign to me. I thought I couldn't be myself (**INHIBITION**) as I had been on an improv stage. I decided to take my own advice. I used my improv comedy training to get me through. I also reverted to an item on my Number One List: My daughter Shannon. She's one of the most important people in the whole world to me. I put these two together. I pretended that every single person in the audience was Shannon and that I was just improvising the same way I would if we were in the kitchen chatting together. Since she is the person I feel I can say or do anything with and not have to worry about what I say, this little *secret* completely changed my approach. I'm sure people felt what I was feeling as I spoke to them: A real sense of authenticity, ease and fun. I was nonchalant, uninhibited and natural; and I just didn't care all that much whether or not I bombed. The irony is that I did really well, all because I took the emphasis off caring too much about how I came across. As a result, the audience got the best of who I am as a communicator.

Your first assignment in this chapter is to make those two lists and to tell yourself that you will do the best you can, but *you will stop caring so much* about those things that don't deserve such intense concern.

STEP TWO

Now that your head is in the right place, it's time to introduce you to a handful of the improv fundamentals we use to make improv folk quick, confident and ready to speak anywhere, at any time. At the end of the chapter, I will give you some fun homework assignments you can do by yourself or with others, to practice these fundamentals. For now, know that your ability to think fast on your feet relies heavily on absorbing and ascribing to the basic concepts listed below.

- **Trust:** Go into every communication situation trusting yourself to say and do the right thing. Also, trust that *whatever* happens in a given improv incident it all will turn out okay if you follow this rudimentary improv precept. I touched on this earlier in the book.

- **Commitment:** Resolve to *stay in the game* no matter how difficult or impossible it seems. Whether or not you like the improv audience suggestion, or feel you can't deliver on it, or the others on stage are troublesome to work with, still go at it one hundred percent. No bailing out, ever. The underlying concept behind performing improv is that you're given a problem and must commit to resolve that issue each and every time. No backing down; that's a rule.

- **Awareness:** To be aware is to be observant. Improv players always observe their environment and watch for important cues in order to play off of them. Watch, notice and be ready to instantaneously play off what is said and done according to what is wanted and needed. This is a valuable improv tool and one you'll want to sharpen over time.

- **Concentration:** To concentrate is to focus. This skill is a critical one. Concentration and listening are closely linked. If you're not focused, you might miss an important communication cue or opportunity. Listening is not only hearing what is said, but what is *unsaid* (body language, attitude, etc.). If you want to think really fast on your feet, your job is to develop a much keener ability to stay locked-in and attentive. The use of this tool is fundamental in every improv situation.

- **Energy:** Without mental stimulation, it is impossible to be verbally quick and agile. Improv players always *fire up* before any performance. To achieve a brisk energy, it might require literally running in a circle, singing out loud, or reciting Shakespeare at the top of one's lungs! When players don't have the opportunity to warm up in a physical way, they do so mentally, though physical activity is a wonderful way to get all juices flowing. Some may sit quietly; go deep within the mind and think intently about things that stimulate high emotion, create adrenalin and a readiness for performing. By the time they hit the stage they are raring to go! Like horses ready to bound out of the gate, they are poised to execute even the most demanding audience request. Without this tool—a strong and pulsating energy—the mind is sluggish.

- **Spontaneity:** This is the heart of the improv player's work. The largest percentage of study is devoted to developing one's ability to stay natural and authentic. Spontaneity has to be quick—so, whatever pops out of the improv player's mouth is almost always genuine and that is what makes the audience respond appreciatively. Strengthening mental muscles, so impulses can fire quickly and thoughts can race, is the goal for all exercises and drills that have to do with spontaneity. Most business professionals that are in a performance situation are typically thinking approximately 35 miles per hour. When you become an ardent improv player you become more like Robin Williams and your mind starts to whiz along at about 120 miles per hour. **Becoming highly spontaneous is how you can operate razor sharp, nimble and most of all, fast on your feet. Lots of emphasis is placed on mastering this skill and using this as the foremost, primary basic.**

- **Listening:** Hearing what is said and unsaid is crucial. If you're not listening to everything that is being said on stage, you risk making a fool of yourself. Pay close attention to what each person is saying—word for word— and also to what they are not expressing openly. This could mean listening to silent cues like body language. It could be someone rolling his eyes in displeasure or saying, *I'm really glad to be at the meeting,* when the tone of voice really says, *What a drag.* As improv actors, we're mandated to listen, listen, listen.

- **Give and Take:** Always sense when it is appropriate to acquiesce and when it is time to take the lead. The manner in which this is done is an interesting dance to do and to watch. The actors are trained to go with the flow of what is happening moment-to-moment. It's a clear-cut rule to lead then follow, follow then lead. In any improv camp, giving and taking is a staple. Look for more of this in your everyday communication situations.

- **Yes, and… Theory:** Always *go with* what is said and done as it's happening; never refute it. This does not mean you can't have a differing opinion, it just means you are always on the same page as everyone else participating in the scene. For example, let's say there are two people in a scene. If one of them starts the scene by discussing where to go for dinner, the other actor would not change the subject by talking about an unrelated topic like the weather. At the same time, it would be perfectly acceptable (according to the *Yes, and...* rule) for them to disagree over what restaurant they will go to for dinner. *Yes, and...* means you adhere to the theme or direction that has been established in the scene. You don't suddenly veer off topic.

- **Adding Information:** The improv player adds something new to the last words spoken or last ideas held and continues on from there. For instance, if two people are discussing where to go for dinner, one might say "Let's go to McDonald's." The other might add, "Yes, and when we get there I'm downing four Big Macs." The other might add to that, "Yes, and the last time you ate four Big Macs you gained 10 pounds." And so forth. As you can imagine, when they continue to converse with this principle in place, the conversation flows like a well-crafted tapestry. Adding information is a natural follow up to living out the *"Yes, and..."* theory. Nobody gets away with not adhering to this rule!

- **Attending to:** An astute improv player always pays close attention to every person in his and her environs. This rule dictates that you always *look at* whoever is speaking. If you're not *attending to* you're not able to increase your awareness and there is also an excellent chance you will miss a cue or opportunity to fire off a quick and necessary (and appropriate) response.

- **Serve and Support:** Another important improv comedy basic, this rule means that we always put the focus on the *other* person (s) on stage and ask ourselves what we can do to *serve and support* each of *them* to make the scene work for *them, not us*. What usually happens in this process is that a player becomes adroit at staying focused and aware moment-to-moment. Because the player's approach is one of serving and supporting, everybody wins, always.

- **React and Respond:** In the player's handbook, as I touched upon with *Adding Information,* it is written: Only respond to **last thing said, last idea held.** Always. Listen intently to everything, then react and respond to the most recent information given. Never say something in connection with what was said five minutes ago, or even a few lines ago, only what is expressed most recently. This is how the improv player cleverly *adds information.* By "reacting and responding" you are able to keep the conversation continuous and coherent. It's another bit of magic spun by the improv player that ensures her communication will never fail. This rule, like the *Serve and Support* rule is dogma! Without this rule in place, the improv player would be all over the place and too busy analyzing all that has been said, trying to decipher what to respond to. Adhering to this principal enables the improv actor to stay on track, and to do so quickly.

- **Be Here Now:** This is the gospel according to improv! You are always *in the moment.* You never jump ahead, nor do you lag behind. You stay current with the dialogue and action as it is unfolding, second-by-second. Anyone who breaks this rule is out of the improv game!

While there are more rules and improv basics, the ones I've listed above will coincide and work together nicely with your new mindset. You will find that when you implement these tools into your communication situations you have a far better chance of being at the ready to handle a situation that you didn't have the benefit of being fully prepared for.

I have often preached that if the general Corporate America populace would only be forced to spend several months in Improv Boot Camp, they would emerge as stellar communicators. They would never lack in the right things to say, nor feel afraid or inhibited to do so. After enough working out, quick and appropriate responses would become automatic to them. And so it is for the studied improv comedy actor.

I have spent most of my life engaged in the study, performance, direction and teaching of improvisational comedy techniques and I am convinced there is no better person to handle the unexpected than the improv comedy player. Consider yourself one of them!

STEP THREE

You may not have the benefit of actually going off to Improv Boot Camp to practice exercises and drills with others, so I've provided a list of fun and invigorating homework assignments you can do by yourself to help you practice the improv fundamentals designed to tone and strengthen your mental muscles. (For those of you who have my *"I've Asked Miller To Say A Few Words,"* my public speaking handbook, or *"When I Say This ..." "Do You Mean That?"* one-on-one communications manual, the homework I've listed in those texts will serve to bolster your skill set as well.

1. Trust: Put yourself at communication risk. By that I mean place yourself in a difficult situation and stay focused on one thought: I rely on myself to say and do the right thing. I want you to keep repeating this affirmation until you finally gain some ground. Building on this habit will provide a wonderful foundation for you, enticing you to move fearlessly into communication situations that are not the least bit comfortable or ones when you just used to sit there, the cat clamping down on your tongue! If none of the examples resonate with you, it's your job to write down a situation of your own, one that allows you to assert your new improv muscle.

Example: The boss has called a meeting and you have no idea why! You do know, however, she is going to ask lots of questions that you don't have the answers for. Although you might find it preferable to jump out of your eighth floor corner office window and hope that someone may catch you, don't trust that to chance. Instead do this assignment. Plan to boldly enter that meeting ready to speak up instantaneously. Go with your gut. Know that you will say something intelligent and meaningful in response to the questions. (Besides if you

opt to dive out the window rather than go to the meeting, you might become uninsurable. Goodness knows we all need those medical perks!)

2. **Commitment:** Make yourself go on a client call you don't want to go on, attend a meeting you're dreading, or face off with a coworker who is bugging you. It is always good to do things we don't want to do in order to break through our resistance and build character. **Example: It's your turn to lead the creative session for the company baseball team fundraiser. Though you'd rather be shoved faced down through a paper shredder—take charge, and this time give it your all!**

3. **Awareness:** Slip into a meeting with the intention of studying one person. Your job with this assignment is to pick up on the visual characteristics and nuances of this individual in particular.

Example: Observe every detail about this person, like on what side he parts his hair, the color of his eyes or his nervous tics (fiddling with his pen, constantly clearing his throat, crunching on the Altoids). Notice the shape of his face, his nose in particular. Don't stare. Try to be blasé. Then go beyond the obvious and see what you notice about his subtext (demeanor). Is he glad to be in the meeting? Is he feeling insecure, annoyed, on edge? You may find it interesting when you notice subtle things about this person you never picked up on before. But don't call him on them. Don't holler out, *Hey! Stop yanking at your tie, you're bugging me"*. I don't want you to make enemies or hurt feelings. I just want you to have the awesome experience of realizing how much you've just seen and heard that you typically miss!

4. **Concentration:** Glance at a column of numbers and see if you can quickly memorize them. If you really focus, you will be surprised how much you can retain.

Example: The recent sales quotas. See how fast you can lock them in. If this is difficult for you, take just 10 of the items listed and commit them to memory, e.g. $2,000 the first (quarter) … $3400 in the second. Caution: Don't blurt out the numbers loudly after you've memorized them; recite them quietly. The

person in the next cubicle might think you're calling your bookmaker to place racetrack bets and, oh boy, that could be cause for getting written up. After much repetition at this drill, your concentration muscles will become stronger. Soon you will be able to stay centered and focused through each moment. Your subconscious has a wonderful way of reprogramming your mind to zoom in and stay present. Rehearse enough so it becomes habit, though. Think, muscle memory.

5. **Energy:** Pick an activity, physical or mental, that gets you going. The idea is to fire up! Talk out loud. Pretend you just won a $20-million lottery and you're shouting such news to the hills. Or imagine you're telling off your landlady. March in place rapidly (knees high) while humming the national anthem. Sing in the shower opera-style, jump up and down on your bed and hoop and holler (I don't care how old you are!).

Example: You're getting your notes together for that big speech. Rehearse it and while you go about warming up, speak as loudly as you can. Just projecting your voice louder boosts your energy level. (If the neighbors call to complain, tell them you're having a hard time hearing what it is they're saying because the guy who lives behind you is rehearsing some speech or something.)

6. **Spontaneity:** This is a very fun discipline to practice. Ask someone to yell out nouns (person, place or thing) then start rapidly talking about that subject until he switches you to another. Don't hesitate one second, switch on a dime. You can also ask someone to write down nouns and stick them in an envelope. When you are alone, pull them out one at a time at 45-second intervals and go off on that topic, speaking fast and nonstop. This really bends those mental muscles!

Example: You're in one of those boring meetings and instead of nodding off for a little snooze like you usually do, quickly throw in your two cents on whatever is said. Expound on your point of view. The boss may give you a high-five for your enthusiastic participation this time!

7. **Listening:** Turn on the television or radio, call someone on one phone and put your cell phone up to your other ear.

Ask the people on the other end of the two phones to talk simultaneously. Listen to all three of these at the same time. See how much you can retain from each audio source. If you're one who has children or grandchildren, plop yourself in the middle of their next argument. Try to listen to all sides in unison.

Example: You're with a client team and they're all arguing over how to go about using your product or service. Rather than listening to the check-signer or decision-maker, see if you can listen to the *Little Cheeses* too. Who knows, the *Little Cheeses* may some day be *Big Cheeses* who could do great things for your career.

8.   **Give and Take:** Go out to dinner with a friend and play tug of war over the check, or take some ballroom dancing classes with someone who agrees to allow you to take turns leading and following. Ask someone to do the "door" exercise with you. You walk in the door, first … then him. Now take turns. Let him go first, while you step back. Do this two or three times—going back and forth, the two of you—soon you'll get a real sense of the symbolism of advance and retreat (give and take).

Example: Next time your coworker wants to boss you around, take charge; next time you want to shine at that stockholder's meeting, back off and allow someone else to take the spotlight. When you get that nagging urge to cut someone off in the middle of her sentence, acquiesce. When someone pushes you out of the way of the water cooler, shove your cup under there first. Soon you'll begin to understand how important it is to know when it is appropriate to take the lead or be willing to follow.

9.   **Yes, And …Theory:** Engage in a conversation with your boss. With every comment your boss makes, think and then say *yes, and.*

Example: If she says, "We need to get the Robbins report ready before we start on the Gavin proposal," you might say, "Yes, *and* I think we have a very good chance of landing the Gavin account." Your boss will be delighted that you are so agreeable and optimistic! No matter what she says, as you continue this conversation, keep thinking or saying *yes, and…*

Pretty soon you will drop the words *yes, and* ... but remain in the habit of continuing down the same path as that of the person with whom you're conversing.

10. **Adding Information:** Using the last example to make my point about this tenet, I will use the prior conversation between you and your boss.

Let's say, in response to: "Yes, I think we have a very good chance of landing the Gavin account," she says, "I sure hope so." You can say in response, "Yes, and I hope so, too, because if we do, I'm going to buy myself a new Rolls Royce." When your boss looks at you strangely, add something to that idea, such as, "Yes, and I'm a real dreamer, aren't I?" The focus is always on *going with* the ideas (*Yes, and...*) and tagging on a comment or response (*Adding information*) that expounds on that idea.

11. **Attending to:** Although you may get whiplash from this, until your neck gets more flexible, go to another one of those business meeting functions and let your eyes look at whoever is talking. When people are having brisk conversation this can get tricky, but it will really help you to become more aware and focused in the moment.

Example: When the others at the meeting are doodling, looking out the window or picking the sprinkles off their donuts, they will miss things that you won't. Besides, all those at the meeting won't really know why, but they will talk about you saying things like, *Gee, I like _____ (your name here). He/she is so polite.* Yes, it is good manners, but it also allows you to be more present with what is being communicated. All this, of course, means you're faster on the draw when you're required to respond.

12. **Serve and Support:** A second reminder, since this is one of the most important rules: The improv player never puts the focus and attention on himself, but rather on the other players, whether one, two or five on stage share the stage with him. Aiming attention at the others enables the player to maximize communication success by catering to what is needed and wanted from them right there and right then to make the scene work.

You should be doing the same! When you stop worrying about how you come across and forego handling only your agenda, you stand a much better chance of latching quickly onto an appropriate response. Those who serve and support are well-liked. Those who serve and support are not busy mulling over what they think they should say or do, they simply tune into the others and respond to what is going on around them.

Example: The next time you have an urge to ponder your feelings or thoughts or preplan what you're going to interject into the meeting, resist. Even though you feel it's only fair to stand up and blurt *That was my idea!,* **hold back. Compliment the other guys for using your idea or say something regarding whatever it is** *they* **are saying about your idea. They'll love you for it! And, you'll feel better about yourself.**

13. React and Respond: Another refresher: Rather than giving in to the urge to say something completely out of context, respond to the last idea said. It's like playing tennis. Get yourself ready and poised to hit the ball back. Don't anticipate, just return an apt response.

Example: Someone in the audience asks you a question and you're not sure you have the specific answer. Rather than screeching to a halt, rally. Play off that question by chatting it up with something like, *Now, did everyone hear that? What a terrific question! I'm not sure anyone has ever asked that before. In fact, I'm sure no one has.* **(Repeat the question.) By the time you get done with your friendly banter you will have called up an appropriate response or reaction in your head; one you can suddenly spew. The point is not to stop and choke on the unexpected. Just keep rolling, reacting and responding, even if it's only to your own dialogue. You know you're stuck, but the audience will never sense that. They only know you are struggling for something to say when you give yourself away. Keep practicing this technique and soon reacting and responding to** *last thing said, last idea held* **will become habit.**

14. Be Here Now: The rule of rules. It takes discipline and persistence to master this tenet, but with enough homework you can do it! Though I know it's tempting to think ahead or lag behind (in your head), don't. You want to react and respond to the last thing said or last thing done, always, and it's impossible to do if you don't stay in the moment. When you stop to think or your mind takes a side trip in pursuit of another idea, much conversation with the others in the room can be lost. By the time you express your mulled-over thoughts, the conversation could easily be well on its way to "Where are the donuts?" However, if you stay in present with what is being said and done, you are far more likely to have quicker and faster responses. Know that if you ignore this important principle it will be virtually impossible to effectively implement all the others I've described. You certainly can't react and respond quickly or serve and support meaningfully, nor will the other rules have much application if you're not in the now. The last three rules, by the way, are probably the most important ones to remember (*serve and support, react and respond, be here now*) thus the reason I have elaborated on them. If you implement each of them religiously you will increase your odds of remaining fast on your feet.

Example: You're so uptight about the sales call your mind is fidgety and flighty. When you finally sit down in the meeting your mind keeps jumping ahead trying desperately to prepare for every potential question you might be asked about the company, your product, the terms of the contract …. Needless to say, you are anywhere but … *there*. Force yourself to scribble down some notes with everything the potential customer says and when you get a *serve* or *support* and *react and respond* opportunity, speak up. If your customer says, "We need 30 pallets of Pickerpucks (your product) by Tuesday," you might say, "You got it! We can get those Pickerpucks to you by Tuesday and also a case of Clipperclacks, if you like." Follow along every step of the way and it will be impossible for your mind to drift. Symbolically, picture the bouncing ball that shows the audience what word to sing in one of those sing-along deals. Good. Now keep your eye on the ball.

Each of the previously mentioned homework tasks are geared to strengthen your mental muscles and make you constantly aware of a different way of taking in and outputting information. It takes time to change the way your mind has typically processed information. First, you have to understand the core principles—those techniques the improv comedy player masters to make them fast (which you've just done)—then make a habit of practicing them. Once your basic tool kit is finely honed and at the ready, the rest is easy. Practice makes perfect, as they say, and practice is what the improv player looks forward to. They truly enjoy running constant drills, for such workouts serve to reinforce the use of all the fundamental principles. Improv players know, in time, and with enough repetition, they will have reprogrammed their subconscious to accommodate faster mental reflexes. In fact, they begin to respond *automatically.* So like them, make a routine workout part of your day.

Let's recap. You have just learned that by changing your mindset (*Ah Who Cares*), you will lessen your inhibitions and dismiss many of the fears associated with your inability to respond when you most want and need to. You also learned about the *Screw It* adjustment. If you haven't done so already, make those two lists: one that itemizes the really important things in your life, the other is the *"comme ci, comme ca"* list. You also just got your hands on a stack of improv rules; the ones that most aptly apply to making you fast on your feet. If you are committed, you will now run drills that engrain those principles into your subconscious so that when you are caught off guard, you won't come up short in the retort department.

In our next chapter we will explore the four-part Fast -On-Your-Feet formula, the one I use when teaching the Fast On Your Feet class and the one that ensures you will be glib, flexible, spontaneous and nimble, no matter what *unexpected communication* experiences comes your way—the ones for which you are never prepared!

It's time now to get to what my students call that magic Fast-On-Your-Feet formula.

"So what happens when Can-Do, can't do?

Chapter Four

FOOTLOOSE:
Doing the Four-Step: How To Be More Nimble and Quick

CAN-DO, CAN YOU DO? – TAKE ONE

INT. DIMLY LIT CONFERENCE ROOM-- EARLY MORNING

Close up: Marvin drained, exhausted. Stressed. Still hasn't gotten the account. Sells big printing jobs. Can-Do Printing has bid on one of the largest jobs ever to come its way. Marvin, the front guy. Colleagues and bosses expect him to bring the contract back, signed. Can-Do in the finals, trying to edge out the competition. Each meeting with NDR's owner, Clemson Rudolph, getting tougher now. Today is the final round.

Marvin sits straight up. Tugs his bright yellow tie. Brushes lapels of navy suit one last time. Starched collar pinching neck. Fits two fingers inside shirt collar to loosen it. Tries to breathe beyond discomfort of it.

Clemson Rudolph enters. Marvin stands. Handshake. Three others enter. Who are *they?* Strangers to Marvin. They begin firing questions

71

TIGHT-LIPPED, MIDDLE-AGED FEMALE
(Direct. Exact)

How old is the company?

MARVIN

Ten, well actually 11 years because …

TIGHT-LIPPED, MIDDLE-AGED FEMALE
(Coldly inquisitive)

Who owns the company? Is it you?

MARVIN
(Forms lips to answer)

OLDER GENTLEMAN
(Cuts him off. Lobs another question across the table)

What happens when Can-Do can't do?

Laughing, except Marvin

MARVIN
(Still on *who owns the company?* question)

John and his brother Bill have owned the company since 1993,
but then a few years ago …

TIGHT-LIPPED, MIDDLE-AGED FEMALE
(Almost accusing)

Ever been late with a job?

Right on top of that line

OLDER GENTLEMAN
(Skeptical and probing)

Over budget?

RUDOLPH CLEMSON
Bullet-fast query

What about storage?

Marvin in freak-out mode. Stuck on *who owns Can-Do* **question. Distracted now. Thoughts of catching up on sleep, what to say upon return to the office without signed contract, wonders who these strangers are …**

RUDOLPH CLEMSON
(A hint of sympathy)

Well, we're sorry, Marvin. I'm afraid we've run out of time.

MARVIN
(Deep fog, mentally. Feeling as though he's trying to grab onto bumper of speeding car)

Oh. Okay. Thanks.

Clemson and the others rise. Begin to exit.

RUDOLPH CLEMSON
(Over his shoulder)

We'll call ya.

Long 60 seconds before Marvin rises to leave

FADE TO BLACK

Poor Marvin. Ditto, I would guess, for all of us have had one or more experiences like Marvin's—times when we wanted to be on top of our game, but circumstances and pressures seemed so overwhelming that our fear and/or our inhibitions got in the way. Marvin needed to be faster on the draw, no question, but because he lagged behind the conversational flow, and because he was distracted with so many disruptive thoughts, it was impossible for him to get with the program. Certainly not the way to make a favorable impression!

No potential client wants to see us lose composure. Confidence, many experts say, is the single most important selling feature a person can project and an attribute that a business professional needs in order to be consistently successful on the job.

Maybe you, like so many others, perform well in some situations but not in others. My goal is for you to hit home runs each time the heat is on and you're up to bat. That may not mean getting the contract every time, but I want you walking away from meetings and other high-stakes situations, with your head held high and with a sense of self-satisfaction. I want you to feel deep down that you did a good job; you did the best you could. I also want you to *know* you were fast on your feet each time you were required to field a tough and sticky question or comment.

In order to leave every business encounter with an unquestionable sense of satisfaction, however, you need to conquer the demons within: Those mental hurdles that trip you up and knock you off kilter. When you're completely fearful, inhibited or distracted, it is very hard to appear poised and secure, let alone sell anyone on your fancy footwork. Your presence of mind, no matter what obstacles are thrown in your path, should make others sit up and take notice. As you leave each meeting, I want you to *know* you've done an excellent job on the floor, and I want those in that meeting to be mentally applauding your smooth dance all the way up to your superb Fred Astaire finish.

DANCING IN THE DARK

If only Marvin had had the Four-Step plan in the works during that important meeting, he may have been able to pull off a big win. He could have at least increased his chances of landing the contract. Marvin, however, is like many of my clients; they just don't quite know the secrets or the tricks that will aid them when it comes time to perform well under pressure.

After talking to many clients who told me they felt like they had been dancing in the dark and that they were chronically frustrated with not knowing how to handle the unexpected or prepare for that which is impossible to predict, I developed the *Fast On Your Feet* workshop. In carefully thinking through and planning the one-day program, I began to rely heavily on my improv training. After paring down a curriculum that would be easy to grasp, I devised the quick-to-learn Four-Step plan—a formula I felt would be foolproof. If followed religiously, I knew it couldn't miss. So after helping students consider a new mindset and familiarizing them with improv comedy rules and tools (those introduced in Chapter Three), along with helping them understand why each of them personally fell victim to becoming fearful and inhibited, I was able to teach them the mechanics of this Four-Step ritual.

Those who have reported in tell me the Four-Step really has them dancing in the office aisles. Yes, they say, it actually works.

STEP RIGHT UP

Since you may not have the benefit of attending a *Fast On Your Feet* workshop, I have gone ahead and laid out the Four-Step program in this chapter. I'm certain if you follow it, the next time you find yourself in an unexpected situation, you'll glide right through it with flying colors.

As you go about mastering the Four-Step formula, keep in mind that you need to integrate these concepts along with the improv rules I explained in Chapter Three. Don't forget the importance of the homework assignments you did in that chapter. Each of those tasks served to prepare you to get the Four-Step plan under your belt.

Once you've given the Four-Step a try, I'm sure you will begin to see how you needn't be reluctant the next time you come up against one of those moments you used to dread. Consistent use of the plan will build memory muscle and that's the idea: Not to *have to* think, but to just *be* when thrust into a situation filled with angst, uncertainty and pressure.

Let's say you find yourself in a similar situation as that of Marvin. I'm hopeful your mind will flip on an automatic switch that kicks the Four-Step plan into action. Later in this chapter, I will point out how Marvin's conversation might have played out differently had he been doing the reliable Four-Step, but for now allow me to introduce you to the *moves*.

1. **LET GO:** This is step number one and a vital basic that sets the stage for the remaining three steps. When you find yourself in one of those *wish-I weren't-here-having- to-do-this moments*, let go. First, take a deep breath (train yourself to make this an automatic response). Next, relax and commit to go with the flow no matter what happens. Even if the situation means you're forced to make an abrupt right or left mental turn (and made to do so more than once) tell yourself you're going with the flow. What you'll soon discover is that most of the problems you've had all along have been related to your tendency to stay fixed on where you get stuck rather than letting go and moving forward. A perfect illustration of that was when Marvin held fast to answering the question about the owners of Can-Do long after the conversation had moved on.

Had Marvin done the homework I assigned you in the last two chapters, he would have been primed for handling the pressure he felt. If he hadn't *cared so much*, he would not have been in a fearful or inhibited state. As a result, he wouldn't have been fazed by three additional people showing up unexpectedly and I doubt he would have been thrown off by any of their questions.

Here's the core lesson in step number one: When you let go, the momentum of the flow just takes you along with it.

You always want to ride *with* not *against* the flow. Remember my analogy about the rapids? Think of what it would be like to be in a raft, spending all your time fighting the currents rather than negotiating them as you bounce along. In my estimation, *negotiate* means to navigate and manage.

If Marvin had acquiesced to the *what is* and gone with it, he would have relaxed and rolled right through the meeting. Skiing is another analogy for the necessity of letting go. I'm not terribly athletic (picture Chevy Chase imitating Gerald Ford deplaning) and typically fearful of most things that require athletic prowess! The first time I tried to descend a snow-covered hill I stopped at the end of every traverse. It was virtually impossible for me to get any momentum to make the turns because I was so tense and rigid that my movements were stilted. Once I let go and told myself *So what if I do break my leg. Who cares?* I was whizzing down the slope like an Olympic-hopeful and loving it. A natural rhythm was carrying me. But before I could enjoy such freedom (and rhythm), I had to declaw myself from the windowsill of fear.

Letting go is mandatory if you want to master the secrets of how to think fast on your feet; and it's prerequisite if the Four-Step is to work for you.

2. BE HERE NOW: This precept, as I mentioned previously, is at the heart of what drives the improv comedy player as she performs and is the basis from which she functions. She is *always* in the moment. If not, she would forego spontaneity and it is spontaneity that creates the excitement for both her and the audience members. **You can't react quickly when you're not in the moment.**

As I mentioned, improv actors practice drills to become dexterous, speedy, and fully prepared for what they can't possibly prepared for. And they *over-practice* or *over-rehearse* to ensure fantastic conditioning. Like a good athlete that trains for a marathon, when the time comes to run the race, it tends to require less effort. That's what it's like for the improv actor. He has worked out so regularly and ardently that when faced with the daunting task of performing before a live audience, his work on stage feels almost effortless. In sum, improv actors always over-practice for the unexpected (which is in every assignment they get), so doing the *real* task always feels like a breeze to them. Each workout drill they engage in mandates that they *be here now.* After enough repetition of processing information in that vein, their minds become accustomed to functioning that way. It may take you some time to reorient your mental muscles to operate differently and to stay present at all times, but with enough reinforcement you'll find yourself going to this *place* automatically when the pressure hits. This *Be Here Now* principle may very well be the best-kept secret of the improv comedy player and the tenet on which they become most dependent. I know for certain it is the rule that enables them to be laser quick. Now can you see how letting go and being present at all times can make you faster on your feet?

3.   **LISTEN:** When you listen to what is being said, moment to moment, both in terms of what is expressed on the surface (verbal) and the subtext (nonverbal) level you also increase your chances of being faster on your feet. Listening is closely linked to concentration, one of the areas of study in the last chapter. If you can't focus, you can't listen. When you have what I term a *thick* concentration level, you are much more likely to listen intently. You are far less apt to drift or stay riveted to one part of a conversation while the dialogue evolves forward. After all, you're moving along *with* the conversation (going with the flow because you've allowed yourself to let go) instead of being on a few-second time delay. People who cling to what *has been* can't go with the flow. Marvin was in and out of listening because he was busy thinking too hard about what he'd just heard. When his concentration turned inward—and when he began to listen to his own thoughts rather than focus his attention on what the others were saying in the moment—he lost precious time that could have been used to tell those in the meeting, right away, about who owned the company and for how long.

As he pondered an appropriate response, the dialogue moved forward leaving him behind. Because he was what improv players refer to as *being in his head,* it was impossible for him to be a keen listener. What does that term mean in improv comedy parlance? When an actor is *in his head* he is thinking or turning the focus inward instead of outward—rather than just going with the flow. Being inside your head can take form in various ways—from assessing your situation (the awe of the momentary pressure), to shuffling through a long list of possible responses. It could also mean staying focused on your insecurities and finding it impossible to get beyond your self-consciousness. When you're under tremendous pressure, that's all the more reason why it is so important to listen. In the improv players' world, if they stop listening and instead get inside their head they will miss very important cues. The end result? They are listening to the internal goings on, not what is *out there*. Listening is a critical component to the Four-Step process.

So far, you've learned that you first need to let go and go with the flow. Staying in the moment bolsters that theory, for you clearly can't do one without the other. When you follow the first two steps, the third step becomes fairly easy: **Letting go of preconceived agendas and being present provides an ease with which you can now listen.**

4. REACT AND RESPOND: Once you have the first three steps down, reacting and responding to the *last thing said*, or *last idea held*, should be a piece of cake for you.

I often find that if I'm not listening to *everything*, how I react and respond may make little or no sense. I mentioned earlier that I wanted you to think about the game of tennis and how a player stands ready, just waiting to return the ball. Conversations are a lot like tennis. It would be impossible for the tennis pro to preplan, before the ball even reaches him, where to stand or whether a forehand or backhand would be sensible action to take. You must wait until the *ball is served or returned* before you can intelligently hit it back. The same goes for Marvin when fielding questions from the other side of the table. He must wait until they are asked and then answer accordingly. But poor Marvin, though he was squarely on the *court*, metaphorically speaking, he was still suiting up as the match was taking place.

If you watch tennis players and others who play sports or who dance (or do any other demanding physical activity), you will see how agile they are as they go through their moves in response to their opponents or partners. You, too, will eventually react and respond from muscle memory. It is when we react and respond from really listening, and we do so in the moment (letting go any expectations), that our responses come more swiftly.

Listening intently is key to your ability to react and respond so be sure and polish that skill. It will take time to develop a relaxed attitude about those situations where the pressure seems to mount, but if you choose to react and respond to *last thing said, last idea held*, you will have far greater success in finding yourself on your toes when you need and want to be. If you react and respond, in the moment, you can only imagine how much tighter the communication becomes—it's immediate, and it's appropriate to the dialogue at hand.

When you react and respond to *last thing said*, *last idea held* and you move along with the rhythm of the dialogue as it unfolds, it's impossible *not to be* fast on your feet!

SUREFOOTED

There is no doubt in my mind that if you follow the Four-Step program you will become as adroit at your game as the improv comedy player is at hers. As you begin to incorporate the formula of the Four-Step program into your information processing mode you can't lose! Remember your other lessons, too, before even trying the Four-Step. You want to take charge of putting in place a new mindset. Itemize those lists I discussed and review them often. Next give yourself the mental note, *ah who cares*. Only then will you have a chance at overcoming fear and lessening your inhibitions.

When you combine a new mindset (*ah who cares*) with the knowledge and use of the improv basics (trust, commitment, awareness, concentration, energy, spontaneity, give and take, the yes … and theory, adding information, attending to, and serve and support), putting the other principles together in the following order (Letting go, Be Here Now, Listening, and React and Respond), the art of the quick response will start making more sense to you. In fact, with a regular regime of drills and exercises you will find yourself running the Four-Step at a rapid pace. Many seasoned improv actors tell me they process these four steps so rapidly, it almost feels like they're doing them simultaneously. Soon you will be having the same sensation. They also tell me that while engaged in this process they feel like they're running after their own minds. That's when I tell them they have finally reached the pinnacle of great improv; they are in the *zone*. When they are where they are *right there, right then*, reacting and responding at lightening speed, it tends to feel as though they have spoken before they think. And they have. In truth they are thinking (or, I like to say, processing information) so fast on their feet that responses are instantaneous. There is no down time, no time to evaluate. They just trust that they will come forth with the appropriate response or reaction.

SAME STEPS

Whether you realize it or not, you have the same capability as that of the improv actor. They are not necessarily born with *fast feet* they acquire them. So as you bulk up in building those mental muscles, fast feet will become habit. Quick is good, you might be thinking, but what about those rapid-fire responses? Do you run the risk that not all of them will be appropriate? That's fodder for a later chapter. For now, however, I've listed a few homework assignments that are geared to help you master the Four-Step plan and get it so ingrained in you that, like that of the improv comedy player, your mind will function on automatic. These assignments are a fine substitute for those of you who can't attend an improv comedy class or an ExecuProv workshop.

1.   Letting Go: When I asked you to take hold of your fear I provided some interesting assignments, all of which are closely aligned with letting go. Hopefully you did them, as they are a wonderful warm-up for these homework assignments. Do a couple of these every day:

- Let someone else drive the car and don't be a backseat driver
- Go fly a kite (really)! Notice the symbolism of loosening your grip and letting it fly higher and farther
- Instead of regular chewing gum, stuff your mouth with bubble gum. Blow a bubble as big as you can and if it sticks to your entire face, so what, let it!
- If you have a musical instrument at your fingertips great, if not, borrow one. Now play an improvised version of any song you choose to make up. This is especially wonderful if you're not the least bit musical!

- Drive yourself to some remote area (one in which you feel safe) take off your shoes (and socks) and run through the meadow whooping and hollering or yelling at the top of your lungs. You can even sing the title song from the "Sound of Music" if you're so inclined. It worked for Julie Andrews.

- Line up a bunch of heavily frosted cupcakes on the edge of a counter. Push them inch-by-inch until they tip over. Rather than trying to catch them as they topple to the ground, let them fall. Suggestion: Put a tablecloth on the floor beneath that counter and grab a big spoon. Cleaning up has never been so fun!

- This last one is for the very brave. Purposely linger a bit longer at a traffic light when it turns green. When the person behind you loses patience and starts honking don't get all riled up, instead just drive away cautiously and blow it off. As they go around you and stop long enough to give you an angry (or obscene) gesture, smile and wave. You can even mouth in exaggerated fashion, *Have a nice day*!

2. **Be Here Now:** Although in the last chapter I asked that you attend a meeting and be ever so cognizant of what was going on moment-to-moment, I'm now asking you to try the following, all of which should feel more like play than work.

- Rent a movie. Notice how "in the moment" you are as you watch it. Surely, if it's a good film, you won't be thinking about other things—how the movie originated, how it was made, how many times they edited the script, who sewed the costumes, what the actors had for lunch or ate during breaks. And I doubt that half way through the movie you'll ponder what the ending will be. The purpose of this exercise is to make you realize how focused you are when you *are* riveted in the moment as opposed to those moments in any given day when you're mind is everywhere but in the *now*.

- Put your favorite song on your CD player and concentrate on singing every note and every word right along with your favorite artist. Make your focus deliberate. Don't skip in and out (like most of us do when we hear a song we like). Make it a duet. Think about how you feel about the lyrics you're expressing as you do this! Try Willie Nelson doing "On the Road Again," or Frank Sinatra singing "My Way." Celine Dion's "My Heart Will Go On" is a good one if you can reach those high notes. Recently I joined in with Sting on "Fragile." We sounded pretty good.

- Make a purchase. Rather than going through the process automatically without thinking about what you're doing, be alert to every detail as it takes place. Take your time pulling that credit card out of your wallet, writing that check; signing that receipt. When I did this once I actually memorized my Visa account number! See if you can stay conscious of every aspect of the purchase as you make it. This may sound easy, but it takes a good deal of discipline to stay in each and every moment, especially with the volumes of paperwork you are required to sign while buying a house or car.

- Go to an arcade and play with a pinball machine. You'll be forced to keep your eye on that silver ball the whole time. You may not have noticed how *in the moment* you need to be to do this. Last time I did this I found myself singing real loud due to lack of inhibition, the lyrics to "Pinball Wizard" from the classic rock musical, "Tommy."

- Take your car to the car wash. Watch it as it goes through the cleansing tunnel. Take in all the different actions the machinery goes through to spray the car, soap it, and blow it dry. You may have watched your car go through this process, but were you scanning every aspect of the assembly line and watching every movement of the equipment as it did its job? You may have been following your car down the car wash line, but thinking about something else entirely. To be playful once and to keep my mind on the homework assignment: I pretended to be coaxing my car each step of the way hollering encouraging sideline remarks like I was a sports coach. Were people looking at me strangely? No. I went midmorning, on a Monday, and I was the only one there at the time.

- Pick up a book or magazine and read a paragraph slowly. Most of us read ahead, or take in a sentence in one mental gulp. Instead, see if you can read each word in each sentence independently and take a brief moment to let your mind interpret the word. You would be surprised how hard it is to stay in the moment and savor each word! Sounds silly maybe, but it works to train you not to lag behind or jump ahead. When you get to *the* and *a*, don't cheat by rushing through them! By the way, I wouldn't do this with Dostoevsky's "War and Peace," it might take several months. Instead go with the sports page or read the directions on the back of a cake box. If you want to work your way up to James Joyce, I say more power to you!

- Make a sandwich, paint a room, tie your shoes or choose any other ordinary task and rather than have your mind on something besides what you're actually doing—that chore—be with each moment of that activity as it transpires. For example, if you're cutting a tomato to put on a sandwich, take note of how the knife slices across that tomato from side to side. Now stay attentive to what you're doing as it separates from the rest of the tomato. Watch each movement as you transport it over to your sandwich. I'm guessing that in the past you (like most of us) were thinking about something entirely unrelated to the tomato. I can't think of too many people I know who fold their laundry and stay focused on every crease they make. Doing something along these lines is a great way to reprogram your subconscious into staying *with* what you're doing rather than letting your mind drift. I got adventurous one day and took careful *be here now* notice as I restrung the laces in my workout shoes, not once but twice.

3. Listen: You began work, in the last chapter as well, on lessons that beef up your ability to listen more intently and completely. I can't stress enough how important it is to keep

doing those assignments, especially studying people and p
up on what is said and unsaid (subtext). Here are a few c   ͻ
now that I think you'll find fun. Each exercise is meant to increase
your ear and keep you far more on red alert so as not to miss
any important cue.

- Take notes on someone's body language and tone of
  voice. Is what she is saying reflected in her gestures and
  inflection of voice—her attitude—or are the two
  contradictory? I watched a speaker once who told the
  audience how thrilled she was to be there though her
  tone suggested she was bored out of her mind.

- Pull up a chair in front of the dishwasher through an
  entire cycle and listen to the various sounds it makes. Silly
  as this may seem, you will hear things you had no idea
  were going on inside that machine. You may not believe
  this, but a friend and I made up a dance routine to my
  dishwasher cycle. It was kind of a jazz, ballet, hip-hop
  number.

- Put on another favorite CD that features a singer. Rather
  than listening to him this time, listen instead to the
  background vocalists only. It's always fun when you
  choose a song you've listened to a hundred times because
  you suddenly hear things you had no idea were in that
  musical arrangement. I like doing the background vocals
  to Aretha Franklin's "Respect" – the *oop* part. Try it!

- Pick a co-worker you spend a good deal of time with
  and get him talking. Ask him what it was like growing
  up in his house and let him digress. Rather than taking
  in the facts, take in the timbre and quality of his voice.
  Is it husky, smooth, raspy, high-pitched? Listen to the
  different notes it hits. You will probably notice things
  about that person's voice you had no idea existed. I do
  this with David Letterman when I can't fall asleep. He has
  an interesting laugh, a whisper of a lisp and something
  telling in his *uh-huh*.

- Turn off the lights, all televisions, radios, *and* CD
  players—make the inside of your house as quiet as you

possibly can. Now, relax and close your eyes. See what ambient sounds you can pick up from outside your home. Is there a buzzing in the streetlight outside your house? Do you hear a train whistle in the distance, a plane overhead, a garage band rehearsing down the street, a cricket? You may have to strain your ear a bit to take in the different sounds outside, but they're there. Maybe it's the sound of the automatic sprinklers. The idea is to pick up the outdoor audio track—sounds that you were totally unaware of up until now. My fave: The wind chimes on my patio deck. Once you hear the outside sounds, check out what you hear inside the house: The heat coming through the forced air vents, a clock ticking …

- Switch on the television and pick a channel, preferably not the news. Turn the volume off. Watch the body language, facial expressions and gestures of the people on the screen. What do you hear in their body language? You'll be fascinated with this listening-to-subtext exercise. It's a real ear opener! For a real kick, rent the classic film "Casablanca." The closing scene with Ingrid Bergman and Humphrey Bogart is sensational in getting this lesson across. I confess I've watched it without sound at least a hundred times (and it still makes me cry!).

- Tune into nature. Nothing creates a more optimal time for self-reflection and introspection. Listen to a bird chirping, a waterfall falling, a brook gurgling, the rain pounding or the wind blowing. The great outdoors makes many interesting sounds; many that we dismiss or we don't even realize are all around us. Communing with nature, especially if you work indoors (most of us corporate types do) also helps you to gain perspective and get a hold of that new mindset. A little lesson I'd like to share: If you go to the mountains to do this, don't close your eyes for too long. I once thought I was savoring the sound of my son-in-law's footsteps crunching through the crisp autumn leaves, but when I looked up a coyote and I were locked in what-are-*you*-doing-here? eye contact.

PLODDING ALONG

This Four-Step program may sound like a simple idea and it is really. Mastering the order of it under pressure is the tricky part. When we work on this program in class, my students tell me that the mere suggestion of the Four Steps and the order in which they should be implemented makes perfect sense. In fact, many of them give me one of those *Ah ha!"* responses as they witness their classmates on stage demonstrating the new program. After class, however, they tell me they are concerned that, consistently using the Four-Step approach when under pressure, may not be practical. Sure, it's a challenge; but if improv comedy actors can do it, so can you. I'll tell you what I tell them: Practice, practice, practice, for I want to see you get to the point where you no longer think to yourself, okay: step one, now two, now …. I want the order of the Four-Step formula to become automatic to you. Realize that improv comedy players are not thinking about which step they are on in the midst of a high-pressure performance, they are just focused on the assignment, sailing along line by line. You'll get there, too, if you persevere. That's the secret.

At the end of this chapter, I'm going to assign a few more homework tasks (fun ones again!) to help you experiment with the Four-Step program so you can be ready to use it in high-risk situations. Before I do though, I want to share with you some *director's notes* I would have given Marvin, if only I could have been there to help him every step of the way.

JUMPING IN

About 15 minutes before the meeting, I would have urged Marvin to fire up. I would have told him to get his energy going so that when Clemson walked into the room with the unexpected entourage, Marvin's mind would already be paused on red alert, ready to spring into action despite any surprises. You might be thinking: How could he produce energy seated quietly in a chair waiting for Mr. Rudolph and company? There are several ways to stimulate energy while sitting in place. One exercise my actors do is to put their hands together and rub them briskly for a minute or two. This creates actual heat, a great signal to the brain to get ready to launch into action. Marvin could have tried that. Also, if Marvin wasn't too loud doing so, he could have started applauding with verve, or he could have pretended to be applauding (his hands wouldn't meet, he would just fake the gestures). Silly as they may sound, these are just two exercises my actors do and ones you too can do to get the sparks flying.

As I mentioned in Chapter Three, you really need energy to be spontaneous. Think of energy like the burner on a range that needs to be turned on (and up) in order to heat up a pan and boil the water (spontaneity). Spontaneity can't happen without the heat to get things cooking.

Marvin also could have done some imagery. He could have meditated on whatever it was that would get him going: thinking about winning the lottery, telling off a reckless driver, hollering coaching tips at a sports team. Any one or all of these thoughts would have actually increased the neurons and electrodes in the mind even though Marvin was sitting perfectly still. I have seen actors stand backstage quiet and motionless, eyes closed—seeming almost lifeless. Yet, when the announcer calls them to the stage, they bolt through the curtains like a herd of wild horses. They are doing what I would have directed Marvin to do: Warm up any way you can so that you are mentally ready to spring into verbal action when the audience shows up.

Marvin had plenty of time in the car on the way to the meeting as well to do some mental warm up. Had Marvin taken advantage of such an opportunity, he would have found his mind traveling at a faster rate of speed. This alone would have caused his answers to come more readily.

Notwithstanding warm up, if Marvin had let go, shaken off any worry of how the meeting might go, and instead focused on the *important* items on his new mindset list, he may have had a more healthy and relaxed perspective. This is not to say Marvin shouldn't have prepared himself for the meeting particulars; that is something each of us should do before we perform anywhere!

To take you back for a moment to the improv comedy player's world; they run the pieces they are going to do for the show during rehearsal. Sure, they don't know what the audience will give them in the way of suggestions. For instance they may be asked to improvise a song, but they might rehearse all the song styles the audience might holler out like blues, reggae, pop, opera, Broadway, rap and so on, in preparation. Now in Marvin's case, he might have re-familiarized himself with the particulars in the contract—the specs the company had asked for and any other information he might have wanted at his verbal fingertips, just in case. That, coupled with his warm-up, would have provided great primers to equip him for the unexpected at the meeting. With all that under his mental belt, he may have found himself performing the Four-Step from rote without any real thought. If he'd just let go, stayed in the moment and listened intently question-by-question (and if his mind was zipping along at a faster pace), he would have answered all of those questions succinctly, clearly, quickly and most importantly, confidently.

Here is my critique of Marvin's responses and a few tips I might have offered had I been sideline coaching him that day. Though I have offered the following handful of suggestions, I need to point out that when Monday-morning-quarterbacking with any one of my students, I always ask them to review their answers (best they can remember them), and see if they can't arrive at several options for handling each question if given the chance to answer them over again. For now, here's an option for each of Marvin's questions:

"How old is the company?"

If Marvin wasn't thinking so hard about how to answer that query he may have shot back, **"21 years," period.** Instead he did as many people do. He began to scan the history of the company in his mind; thinking he may have to provide more information than just a simple number. We all tend to over-explain out of fear, but we needn't do so. Most busy executive professionals prefer we just get to the point.

"Who owns it, is it you?" Probably picturing the owners and thinking he should provide more background on their credibility rather than just names, slowed him down. Also note that he wasn't reacting to last thing said, but first thing said: **Who owns it?** I would have preferred he reacted and responded to last thing said with: **"No, wish I did!** If a split second permitted, he could have named the owners at that point.

"What happens when Can-Do can't do?!"

Marvin could have laughed with them to demonstrate his sense of humor. If he was on top of his game, he might have said with a warm smile, **"Don't know since it's never happened before."** If Marvin had primed himself with drills and built himself up before the meeting—thinking about confidence and personal power—this answer may well have just rolled off his tongue before he had time to process it fully.

"Have you ever been late with a job?"

If Marvin was firing off his answers with speed he may have shot back with aplomb, **"I haven't with any of my accounts, no. Though I understand that those times the company has been late, they have been late for very good reason. We have always made it up to the customer with a discount, hand carrying the goods to where they need to go, or giving them a break on the next job. Whatever it takes to make the client happy, that we *can do!* Would you like me to give you an example?"** This would have given Marvin an opportunity to explain in detail how expertly the company handles pressure and glitches. Most people probably would have been satisfied with the explanation given, however. No need to expound unless asked to do so.

"Over-budget?"

"Only when the client changes his mind. When we give a price we stick to it!"

Again another volley returned with self-assuredness. Marvin didn't say we *don't* go over budget, but he made it clear right away that when clients do request additions or changes, they understand those may cost extra. Returning that *ball* could have also been done with another warm smile.

"What about storage?"

"If the order is too big for us to store, we'll find a suitable place for you to house it until you need it," is what he could have said, but in this instance, Marvin may have had several answers that would have been appropriate. If he couldn't provide storage, he might have said, **"Wish we could, but all orders are delivered to the client upon completion. Now, if you need a storage facility we'll be glad to help you find one."** Again, a real *can-do* attitude!

If Randolph and the others suddenly exclaimed they were out of time, Marvin, in a fast-on-your-feet mentality, might have asked, **"Before you go, can we get that order started for you?"** or he could have said, **"I'll call you later to find out if and when you would like us to go ahead."** Or he could have said something to indicate he wasn't letting go of the possibility of getting the contract. Perhaps: **"Just let me know what I can do to get you to sign our contract, Mr. Randolph. Can-do will do, if you give us the chance."** To really pique Randolph's interest and that of the others, he might have even teased, **"Just let me know when you have a little more time to discuss the contract. We've got a nice surprise for you; an offer I don't think you'll be able to refuse!"** That might have left Clemson Rudolph wondering the rest of the day, *"Hmmm, what is it Can-Do is going to do?"*

Here's some additional instruction I would have given Marvin, a tenet improv actors live by—the *Economy of Dialogue* rule. We are asked not to say any more than what is absolutely necessary as we respond on stage in a scene. This is what keeps the pace of a scene brisk and buoyant. When the actors belabor an idea it weighs the piece down and the other actors and the audience become bored. With too much explanation (a term we call *Going into Story*), the audience will lose interest and the magic of the piece diminishes.

I also always tell my Fast-on-Your-Feet students to mirror the energy of the banter. In Marvin's case, Clemson was quick, pithy and to the point. If Marvin could have returned Randolph's *serves* in a similar fashion, he would have connected better with him and the others. Every improv scene (in your case, every meeting) needs to have a strong back-and-forth dynamic—demonstrating parity among all players involved, in order for it to work out successfully. These are just a few more of the tricks improv comedy players have up their sleeves and, given the chance, ones I would have passed on to Marvin.

The above suggestions are just a few that might have helped Marvin toss back some quick and pithy answers in the fast-paced atmosphere of that meeting. Getting in the same groove as the client would have helped him connect even more. With a connection, he would have ensured good rapport. With rapport, Marvin would have had a very good chance of making the sale.

Don't forget what I stated earlier: We're all selling something and we can't sell if we don't connect!

WALKING AWAY

You always want to resolve a scene (or end a meeting) with a solid and positive finish. You also want to leave every audience wanting more. When you're fast on your feet and keenly on your toes in the process, you learn to anticipate the end of a scene and will seize those final moments to throw out a final zinger, one that leaves the other party (parties) with a positive feeling and good impression! But first, you need to come across unfazed, unfettered, sharp and confident. When you learn to master the Four-Step process that is precisely the impression you'll make! It's only when you balk, clutch, flinch or otherwise give yourself away, like Marvin did, that you lose out and flog yourself with regret after the scene is over.

No more of that for you!

Now, with your arsenal of improv comedy rules, tools and basics, and the knee-jerk use of the Four-Step in place, you're well on your way to thinking fast on your feet, and it won't feel like thinking at all. Do you pause to think about those checks you write, how you open the refrigerator door, how you steer the wheel of the car when turning right, brush your hair, log on to your Internet service? Well, you will be on automatic with your narrative and dialogue, too, once you nail down the basics and practice them until they become rote.

One last thing about Marvin: In addition to him using the Four-Step (which he would have been doing with any one of the answers I spelled out since they were all a very quick, very much a *react and respond* tact), he could have coasted, simply relying on his instincts, impulses and intuition to pull up those rapid retorts.

Instincts and impulses (a dynamic duo and the bosom buddies of every improv comedy player) and intuition (something we all have) are the subjects of our next chapter. I will cover the importance of each and show you how they integrate beautifully with the lessons thus far. For now, however, I want you to take as much time as you need to grab hold of these new concepts and work your mental muscles until they are fully toned and buff!

With that in mind, here are a few more homework assignments that will help you conquer the magic moves of the Four-Step routine:

1.　Try using the Four-Step in one communication situation a day. This might include a business telephone call, a meeting, a one-on-one with a subordinate or superior at the office .... You have opportunities all day long from which to choose. (Don't miss any one of the four steps as you practice). How about that client that always seems to get the best of you? Take this opportunity to show him some fancy footwork!

2.　Even if you're not a tennis player, grab a tennis partner and play a few sets. Nothing gets you in the spirit of *react and respond* more quickly. Second choice: Take a tennis lesson making sure you have the benefit of using the tennis ball machine. Ask the instructor to speed it up. Talk about bringing home the fast on your feet message! If the physical activity of either of the above is just too rigorous for you, sit in the bleachers during a tennis match. I contend that the spectator can always learn just as much from watching. This could be a good excuse to go to Wimbledon!

3.　Listen to someone you usually tune out. Start your stopwatch and see how long you can stick with this. If you can go for an entire minute, congratulations. Most people let their mind drift after 10 seconds. Listening to someone who bores you, drives you nuts or gets on your nerves is the goal because the discipline it takes to stay attentive when we least want to builds not only mental stamina, but tremendous character as well!

4.　Your last assignment has to do with Marvin. Take each of the questions he was asked in the meeting and devise your own answers. Pretend to be Marvin and see what responses you may have given. Don't *think* about this, for the purpose of the assignment is to be as spontaneous as you can *be*. I usually recommend sitting in front of the computer and typing your answers the minute you assimilate each of the questions. Launching into this exercise with a can-do attitude is one more way for you to grasp the Four-Step process and learn to think fast on your feet.

It's time now to move forward for a discussion about impulses, instincts and intuition and learn how these fit nicely into the fast on your feet scheme of things.

"If my wife had given me that tie for my birthday, I would have hung myself with it."

Chapter Five

Hop To It:
One Foot In Front Of The Other

WHO'S THE REAL BOOB? – TAKE ONE

INT. HILTON CATALINA ROOM – MEZZANINE LEVEL – EARLY EVENING

Camera draws back from close up of PowerPoint screen to wide shot Dave, satisfied. Shuts down PowerPoint show

DAVE
(Smiling)

Well, that's all folks. Thanks so much for being here and I certainly hope you enjoyed learning more about the many uses of plastic today and how it can be molded and shaped … how it can be used in so many different ways. So much more so than in the past ten ...

Zinged straight at him like well-aimed Frisbee

AUDIENCE MEMBER
(Smug)

You mentioned how plastic is revolutionizing goods in all forms …

DAVE
(Attentive. Confident)
Uh-huh. Yep.

AUDIENCE MEMBER

Does that include breast implants?

Before questioner's inflection trails off, Dave lunges, verbally

DAVE
(Sans sarcasm)

Are you in the market for a pair?

Room erupts in blast of laughter. Asker was a male

LIGHTS OUT

BOLTING OUT THE GAIT

Dave is a student of mine, who before taking the Fast On Your Feet class, was shut down and shut in, terrified of responding to any communication he hadn't planned for or anticipated.

He once told me that he was at a meeting and an Elvis impersonator showed up with a singing telegram. It was Dave's birthday. The look-alike cozied up to Dave urging him to sing along as he performed "Jail House Rock." Dave lost it. Not only was he unable to sing, he bolted from the room like he was running from the bulls in Spain. He dodged the embarrassment by tearing down the hall and ducking into the bathroom where he hid out. There, he confessed, he frantically splashed cold water on his beet-red face. Now, he tells me, given the same set of circumstances, he may not have accompanied the telegrapher vocally, but he would have at least played along with the gag and enjoyed the impersonator's impersonation.

"What would you have done given a second chance to play that scene?" I asked him during a follow-up session to this crisis. (I had asked him to come up with a handful of ways he could have handled the situation had he not been so mortified.) "I would have begged off graciously," he said, "or had I been quick enough, I could have opted to turn the intruder onto one of the other guys at the table. My counterpart in accounting is a real showoff and I could have steered the fake Elvis in his direction."

"Great idea," I told Dave. "That would have been quick thinking!"

A lot of us are like Dave. Most of us are shy in some situations or just plain uncomfortable in others. However, we, too, can appear as confident, self-assured and as powerful as he now does. We needn't balk, vacillate, get flustered, or grope for a response, ever. Dave doesn't anymore. He told me the guy who asked about the breast implants, by the way, was totally stymied when Dave shot back his witty response. He said the man sputtered in a valiant attempt to spit something out, but nothing came. He shrugged his shoulders instead in a touché, you-got-me kind of way. Dave, terrific guy that he is, apologized, in front of that audience, for any embarrassment he'd caused his questioner. Real class. The man replied to the apology with a laugh, "No problem," he said.

GRINDING IT IN

I try to impress, on each of my students who have trepidations about some horrifying work situation, that there is always an appropriate response. I realize that coming up with it under duress, friction or pressure may, at first, not be easy; but with enough practice, like Dave, responding confidently and appropriately can be confidence-building and liberating! The answers are in there, I tell each and every student. They really are; and there are so many choices, too. **Believe it or not, the answers are deep inside for all of us in every communication situation, we just have to be open to retrieving them. Staying wide open to accessing those answers is the lesson in this chapter.**

No matter how bizarre a situation, whenever we come up with a fitting response, or smoothly handle a situation where we need to fill a communication gap or get the dialogue rolling, we wow people. There is something to be said about the impression we make when we're lightening fast and unafraid and solid; when we're always on the ball!

Dave says he is now more willing to confront difficult situations, head on—the same ones that used to make him cower. What turned the corner for him, he contends, is the rigorous re-training of his mental muscles. He does admit that it took some time to strengthen them; to make them quick and nimble enough for him to have the chutzpah to fly by the seat of his pants. He asserts that practicing the techniques I laid out in the Four-Step plan helped him build courage as well. But, there were a few more tricks or insights that Dave came face-to-face with that sealed the Fast deal for him and that also work for all my Fast students.

BAG 'O TRICKS

I've already given you insight into what causes each of us to shut down (fear and inhibition), and also introduced you to the prospect of adapting a new mindset. In addition, I've carefully outlined the inner-workings of the Four-Step plan to help you get down the Fast On Your Feet Formula" that, once mastered, will help you waltz smoothly through any sticky communication situation. Now there are a couple of other tricks to add to your new Fast On Your Feet communication tool belt!

In review: The principles of Let Go, Be Here Now, Listen, and React and Respond are critical if you want to be Fast. But there is yet another set of components that actually tie in nicely to the overall Fast On Your Feet scheme of things.

This set of components has three parts really, but the first two are a pair I want you to *slip into* (like you would a pair of comfortable flip-flops). They should be worn at all times during all your communication situations. Pay close attention to this pair because they are key to the fourth discipline of the Fast On Your Feet formula (that of reacting and responding), they are the duo that allows you to bounce back without skipping a beat!

These components are comprised of an interesting combo: **Instincts and Impulses.** And here's the good news: Everybody has them! The not-so-good-news is that many people don't use them; they don't slip them on when they suddenly have to walk the talk. But your goal for now is: Get in touch with and be more aware of your instincts and your impulses so you can tune into them in a split second. Accessing them, not stifling them (like so many people automatically tend to do under pressure) is the focus of this part of the lesson.

Our instincts and impulses never leave us. They are very much a part of the human condition and are always available to us. On the other hand, using them when we're thrown off guard or upset is sometimes impossible. The inability to call upon this pair consistently is the hurdle I want you to get over.

Today, due to a completely different mindset and newly acquired skill set, Dave is consistently quick on the verbal draw. Granted, he has learned to choose those moments when his instincts dictate what pithy or elaborate comeback is the right one, or what impulses he should act upon and which ones to clamp down on, yet in any case he never hesitates. He is fearless, confident and self-empowered. He also listens intently to his intuition. All Dave's work and introspection are reflected in a good way, too; he's never cocky, arrogant or cavalier. He claims, though once plateaued out, he now has risen up the corporate ladder because of his ability to think fast on his feet.

When you think of your instincts and your impulses think of this pair like life jackets that buoy you and carry you swiftly and safely to your verbal destination. If you will, think of your mind as a reservoir that is teeming with hundreds of instincts and impulses, any one of which can be instantly reeled in, at a fleeting mental request. One of my students visualizes this metaphoric pair as fins attached to her feet. She imagines them as swimming accessories that help her plow quickly through the rough waters of stressful communication moments.

PLOWING THROUGH

When you **trust your instincts** and **rely on your impulses,** you stand an excellent chance of saying all the right things at all the right times. But most people are inhibited or afraid to let go, so they lag behind or come to a screeching halt altogether when it comes to delivering an appropriate response. We are simply too afraid of saying the wrong thing or looking like fools so, as I mentioned earlier in the book, we filter, analyze, ponder, consider, modulate, mull over and completely bypass any notion of using what quickly comes to mind. It's so ironic since we all want to use our best resources and appear sharp and socially adept.

One of the first things I mention during a Fast On Your Feet class is that I truly understand there is nothing that diminishes your image of confidence more quickly than an awkward silence that just hangs there when it's obvious you're supposed to say *something*. Again, when silent pauses loom or you're at war in your head with what thoughts to convey through spoken words, you've lost the opportunity. And again, you're left feeling humiliated, frustrated and downright helpless. Who wants that? As I pointed out earlier, these experiences tend to build on one another and create a self-fulfilling prophecy. Soon you believe you will *never* be capable of handling pressurized communication situations because, well, you're just not very good at it! I say rubbish. It all comes back to instincts and impulses.

Throw yourself with total abandon into the arms of instincts and impulses! This is major to overcoming verbal obstacles; and as you may have guessed, the heart of the lesson in this chapter.

WALKING A THIN LINE

If the startling question that Dave was asked at the conclusion of his PowerPoint show had been zinged at Dave months earlier (he confided to me over a chilled Perrier one day), it would have caused him to freeze in his tracks and turn bright red. (Dave's dead giveaway that he's out of control and ready to choke mentally is his tendency to turn crimson.) Because he came to **trust** his **instincts** and **rely on** his **impulses** through continual practice, he was able to keep the volley going without skipping a beat.

Wait a minute, you might be thinking—just exactly how *did* he do that? How did he go from bolting out the door and down the hallway to the restroom, to standing tall and slinging a quick barb the questioner's way? Well, it took time and practice and a bold resolve to stay loose and spontaneous despite what he perceived the horrific consequences might be. But it also took a willingness to go with his instincts and impulses on a regular and consistent basis until he finally proved to himself, over and over, he could count on them.

Hold on, you might also argue, couldn't trusting your instincts and totally relying on your impulses prove disastrous? Couldn't that get you into trouble? No. Not if your mind is functioning in the proper groove. Sure, just like you, I know people who are famous for spouting off some wisecrack comment that is totally out of line. I'm the first to agree that mouth-offs can be annoying and completely inappropriate. But, when you learn to get your *game-mind* on (just like the improv player), your reactions and responses are not coming from arrogance, superiority or condescension, but from a positive, authentic and innocently playful place. This is how you pull up responses in just a finger snap; responses which *fit* the situation.

Dave certainly didn't overstep any boundaries in his kibitzing with the audience member. He took time to feel out the audience (instinct) and get comfortable with it before he allowed his mind to access an appropriate response (impulse).

For greater clarification, let me share with you how it works in the world of improv comedy—how the improv player gets to the place at which Dave finally arrived.

Each player does regular mental drills that demand laser-fast responses, nothing less. Every workout session is comprised of a series of exercises that are geared to toughen mental muscles and speed up thought processes and reactions. Most of all, these intense drills push the players to the limits of forcing them to go with their instincts and impulses. There is no way out! That's all they rely on, in fact. The exercises are so fast-paced, not one of the actors has the luxury of thinking things through, and if they do, they risk dismantling the momentum of the improv game or scene. Once dismantled, the awkward silence can kill the piece.

To specifically illustrate what the improv actor is up against and why it is so critical that they totally surrender to their instincts and impulses, let me provide an explicit example. Let's say during one drill, a team of six improv actors is asked to read aloud parts of a novel; a novel that is being written on the spot!

The director will call on the panel of actors randomly to read (make up) various parts of the book according to the audience's suggestion—from the title to the foreword to the table of contents to the author's biography, to the dedication, and then to the pull-quotes on the back cover. They will also be asked to read parts of any one of the chapters—sometimes starting in the middle of sentences, reading one or more of them backwards or translating them into a foreign language they may not know, but must fake. This is only one of hundreds of drills that train them to operate from instincts and impulses. After doing a series of these week after week, you can only imagine how accustomed they become to counting on their instincts and impulses. They simply don't have time to *think* anything through, only time to *respond*. Sounds plausible, but what about spewing out the wrong thing? I'll cover that in Chapter Six since that's most improv actors' biggest fear at first, too, and a valid concern. For now, stay focused on understanding how critical it is to use your instincts and impulses when you find yourself in a highly-tense situation.

Take heart, realizing that you're now becoming privy to all the same tricks and secrets improv comedy players know and use. Don't forget that everything they do on stage, in front of other people, they do under tremendous pressure. And just like each of them, I want you to know you, too, can count on instincts and impulses to pull you through every time. As you begin to become more cognizant of how vital this pair is, you'll begin to gain some pretty substantial ground. Just like I instruct my improv comedy students, I ask that you be patient with the process and diligent with the homework! You're learning what my improv actors learn and I always remind them that getting good at getting fast takes practice, lots of practice.

A NATURE WALK

For those of you who may still be skeptical or need a little more nudging, consider the following: The ability and tendency to come from instincts and impulses is innate in all of us. If you don't believe me, just study some small children at play. Doing so is an excellent homework assignment. Notice how spontaneous they are and how quickly they respond and react with such *honesty*. Most small children are very authentic and genuine (Webster's definition of the word spontaneity). They don't contrive answers to questions. They don't *think* before they speak much of the time, nor do they *over-think* what they are about to say. They just say it! Children react and respond based on their instincts and impulses, unless … (I hope you can finish this sentence, but if it hasn't occurred to you yet, I'll do it for you) unless … they are inhibited or afraid.

Somewhere between early childhood and where you are now, you learned to suppress many of your instincts and impulses when feeling pressured. It's time now to reverse that. If you do revert to the good old days when your mind was free and your mouth was loose, you will find it will positively impact your conversations during stressful communication situations and help with anything that requires creativity. Eventually, instead of saying, *I'm thinking outside the box*, you'll be saying, *what box?*

One more thing to ponder while I'm on the subject: Instincts and impulses have a great deal to do with inspiration. It is inspiration that drives the human spirit to discover medical cures, find planets, compose songs, write books, start worthwhile foundations … what can you add to this list? And, more importantly, what inspires you? Tapping into your passion, or what motivates you, might just help you become more closely in touch and clearly aware of all the gifts available to you through your instincts and impulses.

HEAVY FOOTED

Do you think that the ability to trust your instincts and rely on your impulses under pressure applies to others, but not to you? Convinced that you're the type who must always think things through? Don't get locked into that supposition! I'm going to convince you otherwise. The following test will remind you that instincts and impulses are usually the starting point when handling a variety of situations, and from whence nearly a hundred percent of your verbal (and written) communications emanate every single day. The object and the goal I want you to achieve at this juncture of the Fast experience, is to use instincts and impulses, not *some* of the time, but *all* of the time, especially when communication times are tough.

First things first, though. Take the following quiz. It will change your perception—it will toss out any misgivings you might have about your ability to follow your instincts and impulses when you so desperately need them. Here goes:

INSTINCTS: Circle Your Automatic Response

1. If you're in an elevator and the person next to you suddenly begins to cry, do you:
   a) Stand there and whistle a happy tune.
   b) Check the time on your watch.
   c) Turn your back and begin reading your newspaper.
   d) Say something kind and comforting.

2. When someone enters your office door with a troubled look on his face, do you ask:
   a) Great suit; is that new?
   b) Want a burger for lunch?
   c) What's a five-letter word for doo-dad?
   d) What's the matter?

3. When one of your children, grandchildren or a small child close to you runs toward you with a big smile and open arms, do you:
   a) Step aside.
   b) Start running past her in the opposite direction.
   c) Fold your arms tightly across your chest.
   d) Greet him with open arms and a warm hug.

4. When the grocery checker ringing up your groceries asks how you are today, do you:
   a) Scowl at her.
   b) Reach across the conveyer belt and slap him.
   c) Stare at the floor and remain silent.
   d) Respond in some cordial way and smile.

5. When you're suddenly caught in the pouring rain, do you
   a) Stand there and say, "Geez, I'm getting soaked."
   b) Throw your head back and open your mouth.
   c) Start circling for the perfect puddle on which to pounce.

d) Hunch up your shoulders, tuck in your chest and run for cover.

6. When you're chatting it up with close friends and family, do you:
a) Sit silently with your mouth agape.
b) Play multiple choice in your head, running down a list of potential responses that might fit.
c) Think intently and deliberately about each and *every* word just prior to when you utter it.
d) Talk freely and spontaneously.

I hope you answered *d* to all of the above! If not, I want you to run, not walk, to the nearest therapist. Most of us, however, will have circled *d* to all of the above simply because those answers were not only the most sensible and appropriate ones; but the real ones—the way we typically respond without thinking or analyzing a response or reaction. What is most important to note, is that all the *d* answers were based purely on instinct.

Instinct, according to Webster's, is our "innate ability or aptitude to perform functions without training." Instincts prompt natural responses. Nearly every one of us reacts and responds openly, via instinct, to those situations that pose no threat or pressure. But when we're under the gun, we often change our tune! That is why improv comedy training is so valuable. What improv players learn, in addition to all the rules (as I repeatedly point out), is to rely on instinct every single moment on stage during each improv assignment. They go with their gut. Especially when there is nothing *but* pressure! If they were to do otherwise, they would hit and miss, or fail miserably. Again: Improv is fast-paced, sudden and unpredictable. Instinct to the improv player is like radar to an airline pilot. They function according to it. They allow it to guide them.

My wish for you is that you learn to function by your radar. And you can. Be aware of the instincts that are always available to you, then let go and follow your instincts just like improv players do. When successful improv players tell me they feel like they are running after their own minds, they are responding *before* their thoughts come fully into focus. That's because they let their instincts lead them. For you, it may be the sensation of having said something, then only after having said it, suddenly realize what it is you just said. I know you have had those moments and I'm willing to bet many of them were when you had nothing to risk or lose, when you weren't the least bit scared or inhibited. How about the time your best friend had an unfortunate turn of events? Did you think about the reassuring hug you gave her before you did it? Did you think hard when showing compassion to her prior to softly uttering: "I am so, so sorry." I rather doubt it!

If you use your instincts dozens of times a day, in similar situations as those listed in the quiz you just took (and I know you do), surely you can learn to rely on them when you're faced with those situations that typically cause you to stop dead in your mental tracks.

A couple of chapters ago, I asked that you change your mindset and let go of your fears and inhibitions. Now, it's time to trust your instincts!

A final note about instincts before I move on to impulses: Don't think for a moment that those of us performer types don't have our trepidations, or that we don't second-guess our instincts at times. We do. When I first left the stage and began a public speaking career, I was nervous because the audience members were not my on-stage fellow improv players, those familiar people with whom I had come to trust in spontaneous situations. To me, members of the audience were a bunch of potential verbal free-for-alls. I had no idea what they might blurt out! So, I did what I'm asking you to do, I began the *pretend game* for I refused to live in mortal fear of one of them throwing me off or challenging me and backing me into a corner, thus causing me to freeze up. As I mentioned in Chapter Three, I pretended to be conversing with my daughter, Shannon, using the same instincts with my audience that I use while chatting with her. Until I became completely comfortable before the corporate audience, this trick was my salvation. That, coupled with the *ah who cares* mentality, continued to get me through. Eventually, I was completely comfortable in this setting just as I had been when performing improv comedy.

Here's another realization I came to when first making the transition from improv-stage to speaker-stage: All of us are shy or timid in some way (which stimulates inhibition or fear). Me included. All of us have to overcome those feelings that impede our ability to let our instincts lead, guide and ultimately carry us. So do what I do, choose some type of *pretend game* that helps you overcome your timidity and trepidation. Maybe it's picturing someone you're close to and imagine you're talking only to them, as I do Shannon. Maybe it's pretending you're Tony Robbins or some other high-powered-have-an-answer-for-everything type business personality. Perhaps, you lean on the same instincts you would use while yakking with strangers on the golf course. During the Fast class, I ask every student to write down a mental *pretend* picture of where they are and who they are speaking to that makes them feel the most relaxed and loose. This mental demeanor leaves the door wide open in welcoming pure instinct. So now is the time to write yours down. What little game can you play inside your head to make you more willing and receptive to going *with* not *against* your instincts. There is no right or wrong answer. It doesn't matter what you *pretend*, what matters is that you choose a mental picture that puts you completely at ease. In so doing, you'll converse *instinctively*. Bouncing verbally off of your instincts plays a vital role in enabling you to be fast on your feet.

I have one CEO who gets so freaked out that he simply pretends the board of directors he's reporting to are just a bunch of pals who stopped by the house to hang out. He treats them like he's the host attempting to make everyone feel welcome and at home. It's what we call in the improv biz, my *Attitude Adjustment* or my *Tricks and Secrets*.

CLIFF HANGING

Let's move forward with the second half of the short quiz. This portion of it covers Impulses. Webster defines impulse, in one of the word's list of entries, as "a sudden mental urge to act." We need to learn to rely on impulses because those mental urges often drive the perfect and most sensible reaction and response. Whether you buy into that theory or not right now, it doesn't matter. Just answer the following questions:

IMPULSES

1. When you notice something falling, like a dish sliding off a shelf, do you:
   a) Stand there curiously and watch it descend until it crashes to the floor.
   b) Point at it as it's falling.
   c) Call a friend for advice.
   d) Lunge, reach out, or dive, in order to catch it.

2. In greeting a person when someone extends his/her hand for a handshake, do you:
   a) Shove your hand inside your pocket.
   a) Put money in his/her hand.
   c) Start snapping your fingers.
   d) Extend your hand to shake his.

3. When a stranger shoots a quick smile directly at you, do you:
   a) Stick your tongue out at her.
   b) Notice how far the spaces are between her teeth.
   c) Look away.
   d) Smile back before realizing you have done so.

4. When you see an accident, do you:
   a) Drive by and wave.
   b) Turn up the radio.
   c) Roll down your window and yell, "good luck."
   d) Pull over, call for help and see what you can do to assist the injured.

5. When you find that perfect watermelon and it's the only one left, do you:
   a) Stand before it contemplating the benefits of picking it up.
   b) Lean over to admire it.
   c) Call everyone else over in the produce department to take a look.
   d) Snatch it up and make a beeline for the checkout stand.

6. When you hear that favorite upbeat song of yours, do you:
a) Sit motionless in your chair.
b) Fantasize about how nice it would be to snap your fingers or tap your toes.
c) Plug your ears.
d) Start swaying to the beat, tap your fingers, or jump up and start dancing.

Once again, anything other than *d* answers should alarm you. Most of us make split-second decisions every day whether it has to do with coming to the aid of someone who just fell down, to blurting out that perfect advertising campaign slogan in a creative session, or cleverly coming up with a unique solution to a client's product request. We do it right there on the spot. Quickly and effortlessly.

When most people think of impulses they conjure up a negative image because, for some, *impulse* connotes rash behavior; behavior that can get them into trouble. Well, I won't dispute that impulses can be negative, but I'm referring to the kind of impulses we receive hundreds of every day. Impulses that protect us, stimulate positive behavior, inspire us and spur us into productive action.

During class, I have had many a student challenge me with the fact that because I spend most of my time in the creative realm, that it's much easier for me to trust my instincts and rely on my impulses. I'm always glad to argue that point because I have no more of them than a civil engineer. Perhaps I'm just more aware of them. Perhaps I'm just more open to falling back on them. And it's not that I'm all *right brain*. I have a strong *left brain*, rational side to my communications, too. True, I may not be savvy enough to beat Bobby Fischer at chess, but I can analyze with the best of them. So no copping out on this Fast On Your Feet lesson by labeling yourself a more *linear* type. You have instincts and impulses just like us *artistic* types. It's just that we tend to be inherently more reliant upon them. I'm asking you to do the same. And going back to an earlier chapter, as well as recalling what I said about my own attitude adjustment and pretend game when I'm before a group: Don't forget the *ah who cares* principle. It's such a lifesaver!

STROLLING DOWN THE SAME AVENUE

As I sat analyzing (yes, really thinking through) what I could use in my lesson plans to devise a class to teach how to be fast on your feet, it struck me as I explored the importance of instincts and impulses how critical one's intuition also was to the process.

I don't know about you, but I get *feelings* and *inklings* all the time about things and people, too. Many times, I do what others do and I blow these thoughts off; but I've also come to realize how important my intuition is and how closely linked it is to my instincts and impulses.

I'm a huge fan of Daniel Webster and I've shared his meanings with you along the way. His dictionary interpretation of *intuition* is no exception. He says intuition is "quick perception of truth or knowledge without conscious attention or reasoning." Well, if instinct is said to be "a natural aptitude" and impulse "an urge to act," you have to agree then that a "quick perception of truth or knowledge" is certainly one more integral component that should be added to the Fast On Your Feet mix. In many work-related communication situations I certainly wish I had listened to my intuition! How about you?

It is not uncommon for my students to challenge me during a discussion of intuition, especially the men. They have had it drilled into them that the word intuition is always preceded by the adjective, *women's*. Women or men, it doesn't matter. We all have it. The trick is paying attention to it.

I also tell my students that truth or knowledge, when they're in need of the right thing to say at a critical moment, emanates from intuition; especially those times when they have to quickly choose whether it's better to lay low and say nothing at all.

If you're questioning whether intuition should be given precedence, think about all those tests you took in school. Very often the first answer on that test was the right answer; although many of us scrutinized our choices and frequently ignored that intuitive voice. Those instances were also typically ones when we felt pressurized. Same goes for those communication situations when the tension is thick. How many times do you stifle that intuitive voice, the one that is suggesting what it is you *could* or *should* say or do?

Webster is certainly clear in his definition: He asserts that intuition is that which is known *without* reasoning or conscious attention. Once again, if we listen to those inklings we stand a far greater chance of responding and reacting much faster. And, I might add, more appropriately.

If you're one of those who is questioning whether or not you're equipped with intuition, answer these set of questions:

INTUITION:

1. While driving to work you suddenly decide to take a different route and later find out your usual route was closed due to a detour. Do you say:
   a) Gee, I hope they fix that road soon.
   b) Whatever. Coincidences happen all the time.
   c) So what? I was going to try a different route one day anyway.
   d) I just had this inkling something was amiss.

2. You thought about going to a movie, then for some inexplicable reason you changed your mind at the last minute and decided to stay home. That evening the phone rings and you learn a close relative lay critically injured in the hospital. Do later say:
   a) Lucky I heard the phone.
   b) Wonder how the movie was?
   c) How weird is that?
   d) I just had a feeling I should stay home.

3. You're shopping for a loved one and trying to make a choice between two similar items. It's a tough choice, but something finally prompts you to make a decision between the two of them. Later you notice your loved one already has the item you passed up. Do you say:
   a) Ah, the choice was a coin toss.

b) Just would have been coincidental had I picked the one she had.

c) Lucky guess.

d) Something just told me to buy the one I did.

4. You're in a client meeting and there are a few new members present from management. They start cracking jokes. They seem pretty playful. In fact, it's a pretty wild and open group. It's time for you to tell your joke, the one about the drunk guy who drives through the bank's front door thinking he's at the drive-up window. You suddenly change your mind and switch to the joke about the guy who tries to starch his own shirt. Later you learn one of the new management team members lost a relative in a tragic car accident involving a drunk driver and his slamming into a bank lobby. Do you say:

a) Well, the joke I finally told was much funnier anyway.

b) Gee, did I luck out!"

c) Both jokes always get huge laughs.

d) Something, I don't know what, just made me change my mind at the last minute.

I'm almost certain you chose the *d* answers. Many of us don't know why we go with our *inner voice*, we just do. No need to analyze or question it, I tell my students; better that you pay close attention to it. I find that when most people are under fire in a communication situation, they are so immersed in the horror of the situation that they dismiss that inner voice that had the right answer all along. I know this because I hear many of my students say things like, I was going to say … blah, blah, blah, and I should have said such and such, but I just sat there. These kinds of statements are obvious clues that intuition was at work, but the person receiving it, wasn't heeding it.

RECKLESS DRIVER

I'm not suggesting that any of us recklessly blurt out statements and remarks in any communication situation, but I am suggesting that each of us needs to listen to *feelings* and *inklings* because more than likely they have validity and purpose.

I will never forget the time I was making a speech and joking around with the audience about my book "Death By PowerPoint." I had a line I usually throw about wanting to hang myself with my purse strap from the overhead chandelier, if made to watch one more corporate PowerPoint show in one of those huge hotel ballrooms. This particular night I decided against making the remark, but I wasn't sure why. I just skipped right over it and began talking about why I so disliked most of the ones I was made to sit through. I later learned the woman in the front row who had been rather subdued when everyone else was lively, had recently lost her husband who had hung himself from a light fixture in his hotel suite. When I accidentally found out this information, I could hardly speak. So there it was at work in me. I had no idea at the time why I was skipping the joke; I just did it. I *trusted my instincts* to *listen to my intuition making an impulsive choice* to forego the quip. There was no real thought behind the choice. The entire mental process from start to finish happened in what might have been a total of two seconds. That experience reinstated my belief that not trying to control my communication choices, but rather going with what *feels* right at the time, is always the road to take.

Here is what I find most interesting: When we're under fire, our intuition is even stronger than when circumstances are status quo. It's almost as though some four-alarm signal goes off. So what I want you to get is that the answers are there. If we would take the focus off the trauma of the moment—the unpredictable, the unexpected, the surprises that we weren't expecting or prepared for—and rely on instincts, impulses and intuition, we would probably react and respond appropriately to every communication crisis just as we normally do when we are faced with a physical crisis.

So then, as you go about pondering the importance of your instincts and impulses and how intuition plays a major part in your Fast On Your Feet arsenal, know that each of us has plenty of all three at the ready. Each tool, when used, will aid us in doing and saying the right thing at the right time. As with the improv comedy player, the more you come to rely and trust these components, the more confidence and inner strength you will develop. Like the improv player, I never want you to be thrown—lost for words or stuck when it's your time to speak. Players who are well-trained will tell you that they fully rely on instincts and impulses; that they always go with what their gut tells them.

MARCHING INTO FORMATION

Naturally I have homework for you in this chapter and I've attempted to make the following assignment fun for you. If you do just this one exercise, you will find that you're well on your way to becoming more aware of resources you probably didn't realize have everything to do with you being fast on your feet on a consistent basis.

Start a log. In it I want you to make three sections: One tabbed *Instincts*, one *Impulses*, the other *Intuitive Experiences*. You can choose to make entries a couple of times a day (many of my students do so at lunchtime and again before bed) or do them randomly, whenever you feel like it.

Record all events, circumstances, situations or moments where your instincts, impulses or intuition came into play. Start with instincts to get a crystal clear picture of what an important role they play in your everyday activities. Some may seem rather incidental like bringing your hand to your nose when you sneeze or leaning in to hear someone who is speaking too low. Staying totally focused on this task, and keeping track in your journal hourly, can be positively mind-blowing. Soon you'll begin to see how many things it is you do out of sheer instinct. Naturally, I tried this out before prescribing it to my students and in just one hour I had noticed how instinctively (*with no thought*) I had closed my eyelids to meditate for a few minutes, swallowed my orange juice as I took a sip of it out of a glass, opened the door in order to walk through it, and put one foot in front of the other to get from the door to the car.

In terms of impulses, I did the same exercise. Here's what I recorded in my log book in 45 minutes: I pulled my hand from beneath a running faucet the instant I realized the water was too hot, slammed a door to keep a moth from entering the foyer of my home, rubbed my right eye as it itched, tiptoed across the floor so as not to wake my dog, tucked my feet and legs underneath me on the sofa to get more comfortable as I picked up my Ben Franklin biography.

> It's now time you for to do the same exercise. My suggestion for all newcomers is to focus on one of the *I*'s at a time, for 10 or 15 minutes at first. Gradually, you'll build up to more minutes (and hours). Even after a few minutes, I think you'll be astounded as to how many times you trust and count on your instincts.

Before making your entries, I thought it might be helpful to share with you a few examples culled from my students' diaries:

- Shielding your eyes from a bright light
- Snapping your fingers in perfect time to a specific rhythm
- Wiping the tears away from your face as you weep
- Ducking from a flying object aimed at your head
- Reaching for a glass of water when you're thirsty

I think you'll find the entries you make in your journal eye-opening. You'll also come to the realization that many of the things you do from instinct, you very much take for granted. After you've gotten in touch with how prevalent a role your instincts play in your everyday life, I'm betting that it will make you more aware of how you tend to ignore them when even under the slightest pressure in work-related situations. After completing this homework assignment, I think you'll be sold on how paying attention to your instincts, and allowing them to guide you, can aid you tremendously in being fast on your feet.

I once had a student tell me it was his instinct to freeze when under communication pressure. I asked him to consider that such a choice was no longer an option under any of his professional circumstances; that he *had to react and respond* because it was what was required of him. Given those parameters, he said, he found himself problem-solving on the spot. Frightened at first and inclined to return to old habits, he stuck with it. He confessed he hadn't realized how reliable his instincts were and how much they could help guide him when he let them. He now has new habits—ones that enable him to trust his natural abilities.

After you have made your list of those instinctual things you tend to do in just one hour, and later that you do all day, zero-in on those instances on the job where you did trust your instincts and did so automatically and spontaneously without giving it much thought. Some examples might include:

- Knocking on your boss's door before entering
- Offering your client a comfortable chair in which to sit
- Feeling around for the light switch when the lights went out unexpectedly in the conference room
- Turning up the heat when your office got too cold

KICK BACK

Now it's time to make note of your impulses and also chart how many of your everyday actions are a result of sheer impulse. Some might include:

- Slamming on your brakes to avoid hitting the car in front of you
- Licking your lips when they're chapped
- Jumping off the lawn when the sprinklers unexpectedly turn on
- Smiling back when someone smiles at you
- Answering the phone when it rings

Naturally, I would now like you to record your recent impulses in your *Fast* diary. Once again, I think it will come as a real wake-up call to see how many times you *didn't* forego an immediate and natural response, but reacted without thinking. Therein lies the heart of the fast formula, *without thinking!*

I firmly believe that most impulsive responses, like tying the laces on your running shoes, writing a check, opening the refrigerator, hitting the correct letters on your computer keyboard, are impulsive acts and certainly not ones you consider or ponder before or while you're doing them. They're automatic.

You might argue that these acts I've just described are ones that pose no danger, are easy habits to acquire and are no-brainers. True, very true. But you possess the same ability with your verbal skills—to react and respond automatically without hesitation. But that's the key: to train your mental muscles and your mouth until they're working for you by rote! This is precisely what improv comedy actors do. They train and train and train some more, until they have crossed that imaginary line (the *zone*) where they are giving knee-jerk reactions to what is done and what is said on stage. They rely on, and give way to their impulses under any and all forms of duress. And they do it really fast. I always tell my actors: If the audience can think of something to say in a scene or game, before you speak it, you're in trouble! Given that directive, they do not pause to think, *ever*.

As you get more cognizant of how many times a day you respond by impulse and embrace the notion that you can use this human gift when conversationally challenged, you too, will never be dissuaded or distracted when you need or wish to speak up. Very soon, tossing out an appropriate verbal comeback will be as automatic as taking the cap off the toothpaste. So, don't skip this part of your homework assignment. It's the most important one of all!

SNEAKING UP ON YOU

It's time now to jot down your intuitive experiences. To examine how much you heed them and how much you ignore them during the course of your everyday activities. As I already pointed out, we all have intuition, it's God-given. But using it can be tough, especially when caught in one of those situations when someone says something and we begin to question or second-guess our intuitive thoughts and feelings. When that happens we slam on the brakes, cutting off what might have been the perfect *impulsive* response. It's during the course of all that second-guessing and weighing and balancing that we lose the moment; that we blow so many wonderful comeback opportunities.

As you go about the assignment of writing down what you perceive to be your intuitive moments, don't discount any of them, even if you're not sure. Intuitive moments, I tell my students, are those strange instances when you hear a distinct voice of *knowing* in your head; when something suddenly dawns on you or you get that sense deep inside that something either feels right or it doesn't.

I once had a client tell me he was having trouble distinguishing his instincts from intuition while recording his journal entries. I told him to think about instincts as the things he did automatically without thought, (habits like coughing when you have a tickle in your throat). On the other hand, intuitive moments were those times when his thoughts become interrupted or intercepted by a gnawing *knowing* about something or someone for no definite or logical reason. This student worked as a chemist. I sometimes lay awake at night worrying about him; hoping I didn't guide him toward trying out any explosive combinations just for the hell of it!

If you're one of the readers who need a bit more clarity about intuition and specific examples of what I'm talking about, I offer the following to get you thinking:

- You decide to wear something more business formal than business casual, even though your boss tells you its okay to dress down this particular Friday. You soon learn that rather than working at your desk all day as you had anticipated, you've been singled out, at the last minute, to call on the company's biggest client.

- Though you'd planned to have lunch with a business associate, something makes you toss that usual turkey on sourdough in your briefcase anyway. When you get to work there's a message waiting. Your lunch date has called in saying he can't meet you; he's home in bed with the flu.

- You're in a sales meeting that's going late when everyone agrees it's you who should go to the phone and order a pizza with the works. You do, but for some unknown reason you insist they hold the olives. You find out the new sales gal, the one who ran to the restroom when everyone told you to order the pizza, can't eat olives. She has a violent allergic reaction to them.

- You're giving the presentation on the razzle-dazzle gizmo that you've sold a million times before, using the PowerPoint demo that shows potential buyers that product line. For some inexplicable reason, you pull up the program 20 minutes before you're due to leave the office for your appointment. You feel compelled to run through the show, though you're not certain why. To your horror, you find the PowerPoint demonstration has been deleted. You don't have time to find out why or when this happened, only enough time to holler to a sales-mate in the next cubicle that you need to burn a copy of hers to use for the day, or you're toast.

Got the idea? Go ahead then and start scribbling down your own entries in that Fast On Your Feet logbook. It's easy not to acknowledge Intuition. Most of us take it for granted. But be still and quiet and recount the experiences in your day. See if any of the decisions you made were prompted by an intuitive voice or feeling. Next, stand back and appreciate what an important role this internal commodity can play when it comes time to being fast on your feet. As I stated earlier, the answers are in all of us. We just need to listen for them.

HOMEWARD BOUND

Keeping and maintaining a log is one of the most important disciplines of mastering the Fast On Your Feet skill set. When you can capture those moments on paper and review your journal entries, it becomes a terrific way to re-enforce the notion that it's perfectly acceptable and smart to trust instincts, rely on impulses, and pay close attention to those intuitive nudges. Doing so only keens up your mental muscles and prepares you for the quick and appropriate retorts you need during those difficult, sticky and uncomfortable communication situations. Naturally, you can use your log for the purpose of enhancing personal relationships, too, but remember, you spend most of your waking hours on the job!

Over time and after assessing your entries you will begin to see a pattern. You'll probably discover that if you had moments when you were unable to be fast on your feet it was undoubtedly due to pressure of some kind and your inability to push the pressure out of the way and just go with it. You will also find during such a review that the notes you made chronicling those events where no pressure, tension or discomfort was involved, you probably went with your instincts and impulses, as well as listened to your intuition. The outcome of any one of those situations to which I'm referring was undoubtedly appropriate, wasn't it?

If you do this logbook exercise with enough repetition, it will become blatantly apparent how those *right* answers are *always* there for you by just tuning in and tapping one or all of the three I's—instincts, impulses and intuition! I realize that it's a scary thing to do; to fly by the seat of your pants when you think your job may be hanging in the balance. But then think about how many times your job, that sale or that important communication with a colleague, subordinate or superior suffered because you weren't able or willing to acquiesce to the Three I's, precluding you from offering a quick or appropriate response.

I know you don't want to appear foolish or make a mistake, but if you study the entries in your log, you will note that most of the items you listed under each of the three categories when you did what you did instinctively, impulsively and intuitively, turned out to be exactly what was appropriate for that particular situation, circumstance or moment.

Trust your instincts. Trust your impulses. Trust your intuition. Trust yourself! I will stake my reputation on the belief that if you follow the Fast On Your Feet Four-Step formula and *stop* looking before you leap, you will be nimble, flexible, quick, insightful, spontaneous and as we used to say in the 60s, right on, with any reply!

Start putting the I's to work during a low-risk business situation. When I say low-risk that might include things you say that you wouldn't ordinarily say in the presence of those in your work environment. You might do so during a staff meeting, while collaborating with a co-worker brainstorming a project, chit-chatting with a vendor or dishing around the water cooler. Once you feel comfortable in low-risk situations, up the ante. Go for bigger stakes. Chart your progress. Make note of your wins. Soon you'll celebrate how well you're doing—how habitually you come up with the right comment at the right moment. Eventually, you can employ the same skill set when the pressure is on. That's the real test of course, but I'm certain you'll get there.

I'm sure you may be thinking all this sounds reasonable and plausible, but what happens if you *do* put your foot in your mouth? Then what? Turn the page. That's what the next chapter is all about.

"Quick, someone pass the shoehorn!"

Chapter Six

LEAPS AND BOUNDARIES:
When To Step Forward, When To Step Back
and
How To Get Your Foot Out Of Your Mouth

BACK DOWN CRACK DOWN – TAKE ONE

INT. ICX INDUSTRIES—SMALL BOARD ROOM –THIRD SENIOR MANAGEMENT REVIEW OF THE WEEK

Camera comes from behind. Then full circle. Close up of part in Raymond's hair. Camera pulls back to full view of Raymond's brow, then his face. He is thinking. We hear Raymond's inner monologue in V.O. (Resolves not to back down again.) Boss had humiliated him in front of senior management four times in the last month. Each encounter left Raymond feeling frustrated, remorseful—sorry he hadn't spoken up. But … what to do? Doesn't want to lose his position as head of Quality Control. All eyes are on him. Middleton is ready to pounce.

125

RAYMOND
(Currently mute)

MELVIN MIDDLETON
(Accusingly)

So, Ray ... what caused my team to come in $30,000 over budget? Huh? **(Short pause)** Answer me, Raymond.

RAYMOND
(Finally, meekly)

Well, well ...

MELVIN MIDDLETON
(Mockingly. Force of voice like blustering gale; Oklahoma windstorm)

A "well" is something I'm going to have to go to now in order to get more dollars just to cover your butt ...

Big pause

RAYMOND
(Trying to say something meaningful)

Um...

MELVIN MIDDLETON
(Self-righteous)

Hmmprh

Chalk up one more sit-there, say-nothing moment for Raymond. Too afraid to let everyone know that the overages were a direct result of Middleton's expense account excesses, he lowers his

head. Pretends to write something meaningful on note pad. Rationalizes. Better to save his job than his self-respect.

Middleton continues speaking, but quick to change the subject

ABRUPT LIGHTS OUT

STUMBLING AND BLOCKS

Poor Raymond. He had only a split second to choose between trying to save face or trying to save his job. He later told me, he wished had said something—anything—and he thought about offering several replies at the time, but chose to turn down all of them. Why? Because he slipped into the pair that pinches: Fear and Inhibition. But something else was also at work: Raymond's intuition told him it might be best to just lay low.

He was afraid and inhibited, and his judgment at that moment, suggested he remain mute, yet Raymond's mind was teeming with things to say. According to Raymond, one potential reply spinning in his head, as Middleton posed his taunting questions, was to blurt the truth: Middleton had overextended his expense account, the sole reason for the overage. But like a teetering tightrope walker, Raymond knew one wrong word and he might plummet straight into pink-slip hell.

He also shared his subsequent thoughts of that moment, all angry ones. He considered shouting over his shoulder as he exited the room, "How could you ask me that? You know damn well why we're over budget." I told Raymond I was glad he had restrained himself, such an accusation was not a viable choice and Raymond was wise to pass it by. You did the right thing not to utter those thoughts out loud, I told him. Never attack in response. It just doesn't work. Better to step back.

Even if Raymond had wanted to confront Middleton (and he later did), the board meeting was neither the time nor the place to take such a risk. I told Raymond what I tell all my students: Don't sabotage yourself under any circumstances for the sake of speaking up. I also told him what I tell others like him: With enough Fast work, you'll soon discover there will *always* be choices in the way of things to say immediately—appropriate ones, too, despite the tendency to keep your mouth shut. You simply need to allow yourself to get to work on building those mental muscles so you can access those thoughts that translate into workable, positive remarks. I told Raymond he would have to be patient because having his mind travel in such positive and constructive mental circles rapidly, and pulling up the proper response, would take time; but like the seasoned improv comedy player, he, too, would get there. I complimented Raymond for making the decision to remain silent, for that itself was an active Fast choice. It takes mental speed and alacrity to step back, instantly.

Another point of discussion: There's a difference between sitting mute because you're dumbfounded, as opposed to remaining quiet because you've *chosen* to heed your intuition. It was important to me that Raymond be able to make clear distinctions regarding his on-the-spot choices. You must do the same.

Though Raymond felt he had done the right thing (and I believe he had that day), he also had much angst over saying nothing. We looked at the plus side: Keeping still, while being unnerved by Middleton's words, may not have been a bad choice because it could have damaged Raymond's image had he come off as insubordinate to his superior in the presence of the others in the room. Cheapening his professional persona, for the sake of being glib or exposing Middleton, was not what I wanted for Raymond. I also didn't want him stooping to Middleton's level. Keeping one's sense of self, when it's much easier to play tit-for-tat, takes much more quick thinking and maneuvering, not to mention class and character. For that I commended him.

SHOE ON THE OTHER FOOT

Was that the optimum choice at that moment for Raymond? As he and I began to role-play the scene, we explored all options (some for therapeutic purposes, others for real possibilities). He shared with me several other "wished-I-had-said" retorts. They included "If I had the firing power, you'd be out of here," "I can't believe you'd have the nerve to ask me that," and "Well, why don't we just pull out all the paperwork right here, right now and go over every item!" We both knew none of those replies would have sufficed. My advice to Raymond was to wait until he had a moment alone with Middleton and then confront him, but do it appropriately, without malice. Speak the truth calmly and in a matter-of-fact way. And, as you do, don't hesitate as you begin to speak, I instructed, step forward boldly, no sputtering or stuttering; talk self-assuredly.

What I most wanted to impress upon Raymond is that despite his choice to squelch his comments, it was his stammering and spitting out partial pieces of responses that gave him away. If you're going to remain silent, go all the way with it. Don't make it appear as though you're groping for something to say. There is a lot of power in silence, but it has to be exact. Never let the audience know that you're feeling caught with your proverbial pants down by starting to speak and then not doing so. Intentionally saying nothing, and just giving a self-assured look directly at Middleton, may have been a great option. (Though again, I did stress that Raymond deserved kudos for not blurting out the wrong thing—by holding back what could have been a verbal mess.)

STEPPING OVER THE OTHER GUY

As I continued to coach Raymond, I told him I wanted him to convey an air of confidence, nothing less. For openers, I suggested he start with sitting tall in his chair (he admitted he was slouching, which is never a positive or powerful physical posture). Breathe deeply and evenly, too. You don't want any nervous signals like a shaky voice to seep through, I said. Also, breathing diaphragmatically centers you both physically and mentally.

After some quick comments on body language, Raymond and I then began discussing what he might have said right on top of Middleton's remarks, without skipping a beat and without saying the wrong thing. Some of his choices included "I'll look into that a little further," "*That* is an issue that definitely needs to be probed" or (with a voice in the spirit of James Earl Jones)

"There is definitely a problem with the budget and we need to get to the bottom of it, yes."

As we completed our assignments, I did provide a little more side-coaching. I told Raymond if he really wanted to prevail in the moment he could have busted his boss in front of Middleton's superiors (without it being obvious or actually denigrating him) by playing it coy and asking Middleton if he could have a moment with him. Then, pulling him aside, Raymond could have reminded him of the reason for the overage; put Middleton on the spot and asked him if he wanted him to show all the cards, right then and right there. Or, if Raymond wanted to unnerve Middleton, he could have looked him squarely in the eye and said to him, "I don't know why we're over budget, but you can darn well bet I'll keep digging for that answer until I unearth it *and* when I do, I'll send everyone here an email with my findings!" The latter choice is more advanced "Fast On Your Feet" strategy. But before Raymond could get both fast *and* clever he would first have to master the basic "Fast" precepts. I also cautioned him with regard to *clever*. Be careful not to stoop to any level that compromises your integrity I said, as he left my office. You don't have to sting Middleton, he'll get his comeuppance in due time. Just keep a level head and wear the white hat, always.

SAME OLD STEPS

Since Raymond had had a string of these situations with Middleton (and there would be more to come, I guessed), I wanted to prepare him for what might be in the future.

In prescribing his Fast homework, I told him I wanted him to always remain on guard in Middleton's presence. Expect the unexpected I hammered into him. Stay finely tuned in and ready to deflect whatever Middleton might toss your way. I suggested he think *red alert;* (think tennis). If you do, that will give you the edge. I told him to imagine himself like the sprinter poised at the starting line, ready to push off as soon as the gun fires or like the tennis pro that is ever ready to return the ball. Tune in and *be on watch,* were my admonishments. I also instructed him to put his *game-mind* on and leave it on, until either he or Middleton leaves the room." I shared with him that I knew of improv comedy players who had to work with others in their field who constantly posed a threat on stage. They keep their antennae running high and their composure, quietly and effortlessly in tact. Raymond was to do the same with Middleton.

SPEED WALKING OR BALKING

Though he enjoyed re-creating the scene over and over again (and sometimes used a lot of expletives; but I let him—it was cathartic), Raymond did admit he might question his ability to come up with such fast-flying retorts the next time he was faced with a Middleton moment. "I always feel boxed in," he said, "and I'm not sure I can overcome that." I told him that when he was not so sure he should not feel compelled to shoot something back. Do what you did the one day you told me about. Go ahead and make the same choice: Step back, but eliminate the stuttering or stammering. I also told him not to worry excessively (most people I coach do) because with enough practice he would gain the skill for knowing when to *fold 'em* and when to *show 'em* verbally. I asked that he consider working toward psyching himself into believing he would *always* be able to say something meaningful. I want you to believe the same.

As I bid goodbye to Raymond, I also reminded him he was just like improv players knowing they will be confronted with unexpected, audience-thrown zingers (most of which would leave the average corporate type in a complete frenzy) yet they vow to not cop out. They're used to saying something and they know they can because their minds are always in high gear. If they can learn skills to handle stress with finesse, then so can you. Improv players always convey confident body language and solid facial expressions. They also consistently execute the Four-Step Fast formula. They do this not only when they're speaking, but as they move about the stage during moments of silence. They remain in *character*. Like Raymond, you need to do the same. My final note to Raymond: Study what improv players study and practice like they practice.

WALKING AWAY WITH SOMETHING

What I hoped Raymond would take with him was that there is always an array of Fast choices. I wanted him to realize, though he has the option to step back or step forward, his decisions should never come from a place of fear or inhibition. He needed to believe that his choice would be appropriate and leave him feeling satisfied and complete in his communication.

As I often do with my students, I sent him home with typewritten notes from our session. I told him to review them before his encounters with Middleton as reminders of what he needed to do. Though it didn't happen overnight, Raymond reported in that the list had truly helped him. I share it with you now and suggest you keep it close by if you, too, have a Middleton in your midst:

- Flip on the Red-Alert switch and keep it there
- Follow the Four-Step formula religiously as the scene unfolds
- Tune into the three *I's*—Instincts, Impulses, Intuition
- Sit tall and convey confidence
- Project a strong and steady voice
- Ask questions

One last tool I gave Raymond as he packed up to head out the door: Ask questions. It's a great stall tactic that allows you to buy time, I explained. Ask questions of the questioner—it's a wonderful trick for gearing up to a fast response. It's rather like the drag car racer who revs up the engine to full throttle before throwing the car into first gear and peeling away from the light pole. For example, when Middleton asked what caused his team to come in $30,000 short, Raymond could have repeated the question, "What caused the team to come in over budget? Is that what you're asking, Mr. Middleton? You mean you want me to give specifics as to why we're over budget?" Those few questions could have bought Raymond a boatload of time—time his mind might have used to quickly browse a flood of possibilities until he settled on the one response he wanted. Such a seamless transition might make it appear as though Raymond hadn't skipped a beat at all, instead it would have seemed as though he was simply trying to clarify Middleton's intent before offering up a reply. Talk about coming across with confidence, conviction and poise!

WHICH WAY DO WE GO?

In the end, it's all about choice. Each of us must decide what path to walk in our communication. Should we buy time, step back and remain silent, or step forward and speak convincingly? My preference, as I've said all along, is to step forward; to say *something* in every instance. In the end, for all of us, it's our call. The ability to make a quick, clear choice, in and of itself, requires rapid thinking!

For fun, and to keep Raymond from falling into the trap of stepping back, I gave him the same list I give all my students who tend to retreat or stammer as Raymond did in Middleton's presence. The list, while tongue in cheek, is illuminating and points out what I believe are the few specific and *only* times when I think, it's not only appropriate, but best to step back completely and say nothing:

- You're being held at gunpoint
- The police have just finished reading you your Miranda rights.
- Your teenager insists on continuing a ridiculous argument with you.
- You're at a wedding ceremony and you don't like your best friend's almost-husband (or wife), and the person officiating asks, "Is there any person present who thinks this man and woman should not be married to one another?"
- Someone in the room says "And now for a moment of silence."
- The judge lets you know if you say one more thing out of turn he is going to fine you.
- You're playing hide and seek and you're not it.

***

IT ALL ADS UP – TAKE ONE

INT. LUNCH ROOM – SMULTZ AND SCHULTZ ADVERTISING – HIGH NOON

Half-dozen ad execs seated at the office lunch table.

CLOSE UP: Account Executive Danowski enters with big burger. Camera follows him. He sits. Takes bite. Notices fellow AE, Dawson, wearing familiar neon neckware.

DANOWSKI
(Upbeat. Smug. Playful)

If my wife had given me that tie for *my* birthday, Dawson, I would have hung myself with it! **(Bends over with laughter at his clever one-liner)**

Others seated stop chewing. Collective gasp.

DANOWSKI
(Looks around, puzzled)

Guy seated next to him slips him note. It reads: Dawson's wife was just diagnosed with breast cancer.

DANOWSKI
(Doesn't skip a beat)

Say, how about if I just take off my belt so you can flog me with it?!

DAWSON
(Smiles appreciatively. Chuckles slightly)

Yeah. Good idea.

DANOWSKI
(Only a half-beat follows that, then, quietly)
Sorry Dawson. **(Sincere)** I had no idea Danielle was ill. I'm so
sorry. Truly sorry.

DAWSON

Thanks ...

WALKING A FINE LINE

Danowski was fairly quick on the draw and thank goodness
he dove for a humorous aside, for the tension in the room was
pretty thick. Had Danowski just stepped back and sat there after
making the crack about the tie, the discomfort in the room could
have hung over that lunch room like the pall that lingers after a
nuclear blast. Although Danowski had bombed with his opening
remark, at least he was quick to recover.

Danowski later told me that the Dawson incident was one
of the most embarrassing and uncomfortable moments of his
professional life. He was so remorseful. But lucky for him, I said,
he was willing to *step forward* rather than allow fear or inhibition
in the moment to silence him.

Unlike Raymond, Danowski dove right in and went with his
instincts and impulses—and leaned on his intuition—as a means
to salvage and repair the moment. And it worked. Had he simply
stepped back or offered a limp apology, I'm convinced that the
atmosphere in the room would have remained tense or at least
awkward—especially in that setting, because the lunch meeting
was a creative brainstorming session. Without Danowski's quick
wit, the others seated around the table may have remained as
skittish as spies at a photo shoot.

WALKING AWAY

When working with Danowski, he told me that after that
incident he had strongly considered giving up his propensity for
the quick banter and the pithy barbs he was known for. He had
second thoughts about wielding his trademark funny stuff even

though his colleagues always came to rely on him for bringing life to any party (and meeting). He was worried that living up to that expectation might not be worth the risk.

Subdued, during his first private coaching session with me, he finally quoted the lead character from the "Dragnet" television series, by saying, "I'm just going to give them the facts, ma'am, nothing but the facts ... for ever more." "No you're not," I shot back. "You're going to stay fast on your feet *especially* when you trip on them!"

I asked him how often he found himself in communication jams similar to that of the one with Dawson. "I can't even remember ... not very often," he said. Then I asked if he'd ever had an incident when he *couldn't* rebound; when he had absolutely *nothing* to say. "No," he said, "never. But maybe it's time to rethink spouting off." "No, please don't go there," I said. "Don't give up a gift that others would clamor for! Don't even think about stepping back! There are people who would give anything to be able to walk in your shoes," I finally convinced him.

WALKING BACKWARDS

I told Danowski that the majority of people who came to counsel with me had the opposite problem that he did; they couldn't call up anything to say even when they wanted to. He laughed because he was always flooded with ideas of things to say on the spot; in fact, he often had trouble selecting which glib response to articulate. *Hallelujah*, I thought. That's a happy problem. So, I reiterated to him that he should never think of going backwards—walking away—from one of his greatest communication gifts. I told him to trust that he would always have a viable *save* even if and when he messed up.

I felt safe giving these director's notes because I knew Danowski was as skilled as many of my best improv players. He was never at a loss for words and whenever he threw something out, hardly a full beat had passed. Just like the really fast improv player, he was always right on top of the other person's line.

What if you accidentally put your feet in your mouth? We all do it occasionally. I say that with conviction because I don't care who you are and how skilled you may be as a communicator, the day will come when you just may say the wrong thing at the wrong time. Accepting that this can happen, and will, and knowing that once you practice the Fast On Your Feet tenets you will *always* be able to bail yourself out with an appropriate follow-up remark to your faux pas, are two of the most important points in this book.

Communication mistakes happen and they always will. *The key is not to allow any one of them to throw you or shut you down when they do.* Instead rely on the given that you will always find a graceful way to get your feet out of your mouth. It could be a knee-jerk retort like Danowski's, or a simple apology. Or both.

BACKING OFF

If you're someone who would rather step back than make a mistake, you must work to get past that. You want to build the courage to stay in the game even when the game proves risky, and even when you've had some setbacks. Unlike Danowski who had something to say, most people in his predicament would have just sat there with a mouthful of moccasin. That I know. Danowski was lucky. He had the Fast gift. The last thing I wanted him to do was to throw it away! Thank goodness I finally talked him out of it.

If you're the type that has a similar gift, but gave it up long ago for the sake of corporate safety, please reconsider. I mentioned earlier that most children are free and spontaneous, but somewhere along the way—perhaps because of a "Danowski Moment"—they began to shut down. With enough similar experiences, children build on their reluctance to use the fast verbal reflexes with which they were imbued and therein lies the tragedy. Children become adults and adults begin to care too much! (Remember the *ah, who cares* lesson earlier in the book.) Don't fall into that trap especially if you have a natural ability to be fast verbally.

If you're inclined to step back because of a handful of embarrassing or humiliating moments, don't do it. Just pick up the pieces and move on. Strive to move forward with your conversation no matter how uncomfortable the moment and no matter how you may have temporarily inserted your foot in your mouth. Resolving to keep your gift in tact and the willingness to use it, despite any mistakes, is the true mark of a great improv performer.

Perhaps you have found yourself in a similar predicament as that of Danowski. If so, cut yourself some slack just like Danowski did.

As I *deconstructed* the scene with Dawson, he was quick to agree that he had no way of knowing that Danielle Dawson was ill. I also got him to admit that he knew many people who found themselves in similar jams. Then I asked him to tell me what he felt for the person with his foot in his mouth when he witnessed such a situation. He was quick to offer that he was always rooting for them to rebound and recover. That said, I knew he got my drift.

PUT YOUR FEET UP

To set him at ease, I told Danowski a few stories of my own, times when I had put my foot in my mouth and also about times when I had seen others do it. It had happened to a good friend of mine, Toni (another ad agency type). We worked together. It was her custom to come across as bold and forthcoming, speaking up whenever she felt like it. One day I recall her saying loudly to our boss, "You look glum. What's your problem?" Then sarcastically, "You look like you just went to a funeral!" Well, he had. Our boss had lost one of his best friends in a tragic accident and he just stopped by the agency for a moment to pick up his mail. He told her point blank that's exactly where he had been. Toni sat frozen. She was mortified. Red-faced and wide-eyed, she was at a complete loss for words. When a few hours had passed, she asked me why I thought she found it impossible to speak. I glibly told her I thought it was because her tongue had gotten tangled around her stiletto heels. Later, of course, she thought of a zillion things to say, but the moment was gone. It was too late. It took Toni time to recover from that incident just like Danowski with his, but she had. She refused to give up her hallmark zingers all because of that negative experience. She told me years later that she easily could have gone the other way; she could have retreated into herself and stifled all her spontaneous thoughts, but she had had far more successes than failures and she wasn't about to give up on taking a verbal chance.

Like Toni and Danowski, I've had my own embarrassing moments. I once went into a store, got to chit-chatting with a sales clerk, and asked when her baby was due. Behind a sinister stare she told me she wasn't pregnant. Holy Cow! At first I gasped and just stood there. Then I told her she could charge me double if she wanted. She laughed. We then got into a discussion about weight loss and what a constant battle it was. I left her with a heartfelt apology. She graciously accepted it. I made a point of stopping in to see her just to say hello whenever I was in the mall. We became friendly and she wound up referring her brother to me who became a very good client.

Another time, in college, I was trying to gather fellow students to come to a pep rally for the football team (I was a pom-pom girl). One guy told me he couldn't come because he had a class. I suggested he ditch it. I told him that's what all the others were doing. Not a good thing to say because I quickly learned he was the instructor. (He looked so young!) So, yes, I too have had my share of open-mouth-insert-foot moments.

My point is this: All of us will have times when we blurt something out spontaneously, then realize we've made a big mistake. That's Communication Reality. But, it is most important that we remain willing to jump on top of such verbal mistakes with quick comebacks. Sometimes a spontaneous apology might be the correct choice. Such was the case with the not-really-pregnant sales clerk. Can you imagine the outcome of that situation had I said nothing at all? And you may be wondering, how did I cover my mistake with the college instructor? I immediately told him what a fool anyone would be to miss *his* class. I threw in a wink. (This was before sexual harassment became vogue or such gestures became politically incorrect!)

NO FOOTPRINTS LEFT BEHIND

Enough about me. Let's get back to the situation with Danowski. His initial comment around the lunch table was an innocent one, just a quick little jab at his friend and colleague. He had no idea at first he had made a foolish mistake. Danowski was clueless. Not until Danowski was passed the note did he know his prankish remark was totally inappropriate for that moment or that his fellow colleague was suffering. Often that is the case with many of us. We blurt something out, very naively, only to get new information that indicates we've made a major mistake.

For most of us, stepping on someone's emotional toes is an accident because we have no advance warning as to a person's circumstances. My friend Toni had no idea our boss's friend had passed away; nor did I know the guy I was trying to lure to the pep rally was the teacher of the class I was suggesting everyone ditch. You can't possibly know many of these things in advance. Shoving your foot in your mouth is bound to happen sometimes. What is important is your ability to yank that foot out. We tend to be very forgiving of those who have the talent to quickly recover from faux pas. It's impressive to observe when someone rebounds with confidence and grace. So, if you're like Danowski, offering up a playful and friendly hello, but end up with hoof-in-mouth dis-ease, let your mind go, let your impulses kick in, and say what comes naturally. If you follow up quickly, chances are it will be the right thing to say.

I don't know the statistics, but I would hazard a guess that in the business world, faux pas are passed around as randomly as post-its! So, if you're among the crowd that has made verbal mistakes, don't beat yourself up, and don't shut down. Know that with the Fast principles at work you can quickly rebound. And whatever you do, don't sit on your gift of gab. Everyone will lose out!

TRAMPLERS

I will agree that while there are the innocent types like Danowski and Toni, there are also those who just blurt things out without any consideration for others. I have overheard many people who have done this. One particular incident sticks out in my mind. I was leaving a meeting with a potential client and on my way to the lobby exit. Laughingly, a guy peered over his office cubicle partition and addressed his coughing co-worker who apparently suffered from chronic asthma, with this: "Hey, Jack, you look like the Pillsbury Dough Boy, the one in that 'Ghostbusters' movie. Maybe you ought to cut back on the Prednisone."

Everyone I passed within earshot in the hallway cringed. So, yes, there are those who may not mean to be cruel (they're just verbal klutzes or only trying to be funny or cute), but they have poor judgment. In any event, whether it's the Man-In-The-Cubicle, or someone you know, such comments can certainly hurt, embarrass or upset people. Exercise good judgment, always. Good judgment is linked closely to your intuition. So tune in and you're less likely to be a bonehead like Cubicle-Man.

The reality is none of us can avoid an occasional *trample* when we're open and highly communicative, but all of us can quickly repair one—jump right on top of our mistake and make up for it like Danowski did. In the case of misguided remarks like those coming from The-Man-In-The-Cubicle, we also have the power and the ability to cover for those folks.

So consider this: When someone makes a blunder or a tasteless comment, keep in mind it doesn't always have to be up to the person who did it to save the day. Anyone can step forward and help out. For instance, had Danowski froze in his verbal tracks, another person at that table could have countered his remark with a "save." Same goes for Cubicle-Man. So, if you're one of those just sitting on the sidelines, get in gear with your new Fast On Your Feet tool kit so you can jump in when a communication rescue is desperately needed.

WALK A WHILE IN HIS SHOES

During my "How To Think Fast On Your Feet" class I always ask my students to spontaneously (I have a timer going) write down what they may have said had they been seated around the table with Danowski. Also, what they could have said if they were within earshot of Cubicle-Man. The assignment is called: Save the day! The following is a sampling of quick answers drummed up by some of my students. You'll note they are also asked to identify the attitude or tone with which the remark is given. First those pertaining to Dawson:

- Supportive: "Hey, that tie speaks to me, Dawson. It says: 'Get out of the way, creative genius at work."

- Playful: "Are you kidding? That tie calls this meeting to order."

- Complimentary: "I love the tie Dawson, it sets off your eyes … shows off their sparkle and energy. Good choice. Here's to Danielle!"

- Protective: "Hey, get back, Loretta. I was just about to ask if I could borrow it."

- Encouraging: "I think you should wear that tie to the Mear Motors presentation next week! Nothing says 'Welcome' more than energetic neckwear!"

Here are a handful of choices gleaned from student papers that apply to Jack:

- Complimentary: "You're still the best looking guy in R & D."

- Humorously: (To Cubicle-Man) "Well if Jack is dough, you're toast!"

- Reassuringly: "What's that old saying of my mother's? Sticks and stones can break your bones, but names will never hurt me!"

- Defensively: "Hey Jack, pass the Prednisone. Let's see what he (Cubicle-Man) looks like after a few days on it."

- Warningly: "Speaking of the "Ghostbuster" movie, we all remember what happened to those who got in the way of the Pillsbury Dough Boy, *don't* we?"

SIDE STEPPING

After my students offered their choices, I agreed that many of them were humorous, but I told them I wanted them to consider that with future assignments (and we would be doing several) there would be one rule. I told them their comebacks could not be malicious, cutting, caustic, cruel or demeaning to others. I told them get-your-foot-out-of-your-mouth-fast strategies might pass with just a hint of sarcasm—those were sometimes acceptable if self-directed. So long as your comments don't hurt the other party, or the others in the room, being a little smart alecky could go a long way. I pointed out that Danowski's comeback fit tightly into that category.

I also share with my Fast group what I share in my "What's So Funny?" class (where students are taught to use humor and good storytelling in their speeches and presentations): Keep your mind in an appropriate place—train it to go there when under pressure just like improv players do when they train. And when in doubt, always put the joke on yourself. That's precisely what Danowski did. When he tossed out the zinger about Dawson flogging him, it was a self-deprecating remark and one that couldn't possibly injure anyone else in the room, only him (and Danowski wasn't about to take himself personally!!).

I also tell my students, actors and business folk alike, to use common sense and good taste. Most of us know the difference between what is tasteful and what is not. If you're not sure, call your mother and ask for that list of admonishments she hammered into you before you even got to kindergarten. Two come to mind: "Do unto others as you would have them do unto you" and "If you can't say anything nice, don't say anything at all." Can you think of others? Good. Write them down in your Fast journal.

As you go about playing with what *you* would have said in either of the instances described above (your homework), let the rules I just mentioned guide you. Put the joke on yourself and you can't go wrong. Many great stand-up comedians ensure their success with their audiences when they choose not to insult *them*, but rather pick on themselves. If you get into the habits of processing your thoughts with the idea that you will not bash or trash anyone, your Instincts and Impulses will grab for those right answers; the ones that fit appropriately. If you currently have the bad habit of always putting down the other person with your snappy comebacks, break the cycle, just like you may have done with other automatic and poor verbal habits. Swearing is one such example. Can you think of others?

Another of your fun homework assignments is to take in a stand-up comedy showcase. Either watch one on cable television or see one live. Notice the material the comics use. You'll find the ones who pick on themselves are rather endearing. Often, the caustic ones make you feel uncomfortable. Whatever it is you notice, jot down those observations in your journal.

POWER WALKING

You can do wonderful things conversationally to repair the damage or salvage the moment, just as Danowski had done, and my students—the ones who offered suggestions for Jack's fellow workers. You could be the one making the mistake or taking the discomfort out of the situation by covering for one (saving the day)! Either way, *you* too can *save the day.*

Perhaps you've spent more time in Dawson's chair—you were at the effect of someone else's comment—and just sat there, stunned, so you stepped back rather than responded. Maybe you were the perpetrator like Cubicle-Man or Danowksi, or Toni. Or perhaps you were somehow caught in the middle, like me, passing by Jack's office—the innocent bystander. The goal once again, under any and all uncomfortable communication circumstances, is to get you to step forward. I believe it's always the better way to go. Opt for a quick rebound in order to bring the situation back into balance. Danowski did it. His comment about Dawson flogging him was a quick and witty dig that seemed to fit the situation and it broke the ice. It also caused Dawson to laugh, if even only slightly. Given Dawson's despondency over his wife's condition, it was certainly a welcome, albeit, fleeting time-out.

Another instruction: Don't collect (and store) a bag of potential comebacks to throw out when you make a mistake, or take a great line you've overheard and try to make it your own. It never works. Take Danowski's remark. It certainly wasn't pre-thought; it was spontaneous and authentic to that situation. There is always something very funny about things said that are obviously spontaneous. This is exactly why improv players are so successful. They are always very spontaneous. They wouldn't dream of saving up a line from a previous show, or stealing a line from another actor and using it as their own when the opportunity presents itself. Any audience can tell the difference between a real on-the-spot quip and one that has been recycled. I know people who offer an automatic reply to any uncomfortable situation as a means of something to say, like the guy at the hotel chain meetings who said after every foolish remark, "Well, just call me the *Office Dunce*! The first time it was funny because he just blurted it out. After that, the line lost its luster.

STEPPING HIGH

Now for my next point and a major lesson in this book: Danowski quickly recaptured the moment—stepped up—when he used humor to respond to one of those *don't-know-what-to-say-when* ... moments. Humor, I have found (and have proved) is one of the most powerful communication tools of all, especially when used during sticky situations. Humor is always a positive way to save the day, for if handled appropriately, it can diffuse anger, neutralize tension, annihilate friction, and repair communication transgressions. Since laughter makes everyone feel better (neurologists tell us it stimulates those mental juices and endorphins), it can always lift the spirits. It also helps keep everyone who is involved in uneasy dialogue in touch with a healthy perspective.

In addition to "How To Think Fast On Your Feet (Without Putting Them in Your Mouth)," my ExecuProv training company offers another class: "Humor in the Workplace." This workshop deals solely with helping people discover, strengthen and use their mental humor muscles in the face of difficult communication situations on the job. Students love this class because they spend the entire day handling one tough scene after another. They are allowed *only* to use humor to communicate their concerns, frustrations, fears and needs. I am constantly amazed at how powerful their communication becomes and how positive the outcome when tense and angry responses are replaced with humorous ones.

I feel strongly that there is nothing more bonding than humor where tension is present, or where the communication situation has gone awry. Humor is an awesome and potent tool; one that should be carefully sharpened for regular use. Personally, when used in good taste, I've yet to see humor fail. Talk about *stepping up*!

My wish is that you tone up your humor muscles by engaging in any activity that makes you laugh. For homework you can make a list of places to go, movies to see, events to take in (like that go-see-a-stand-up-comic-assignment for one) that are presented for the humorous pleasure of the audience. Reading well-done humorous literature like Erma Bombeck and Art Buchwald are two ways I exercise my humor muscle. Writing a satirical sketch is another. Doing both of these homework tasks keep my mental muscles buff!

As you do your other Fast drills, spend some time creating and enjoying humor. Doing so is a way of stuffing more arsenal into your Fast bag of tricks.

STEPPING UP HOMEWORK

In addition to coming up with comments you think would have worked as comebacks in the Danowski and Jack situations, I'm now going to ask that you write down a few of your most memorable workplace faux pas—either those you have made yourself or those you've witnessed others making. When you've finished, provide at least four potential responses you think could have worked to mitigate the communication damage by stepping up. Now do this exercise once again, only this time by using only humorous responses. If you're at a loss for recalling such communication situations to use for this exercise (perhaps you're blocking them), here are a few I've collected. Now, write down what your comebacks would be. Set a timer so you're forced to respond quickly.

- The guy, who during a training session for lower management says, "I don't know who did this PowerPoint show, but this is the worst thing I've been given to use as a teaching aid! It's cluttered, it's junky, geez ... I apologize that you have to look at this ..." Unbeknownst to the trainer, the guy he had teamed up with, his immediate supervisor who was seated to his right, interrupts him with an "I did." It stops the show in more ways than one. Okay, what would you say?

- The guy who says to his direct report as they get off the plane in Sacramento from Los Angeles to give a sales presentation, "As soon as you change into your meeting suit, Kendrick, we'll head down to the Pacific Room so I can introduce you to the Big Cheese." The guy didn't know that his subordinate did not have another suit, that what he was wearing was what he intended to wear to the meeting. "Actually my uncle is the Big Cheese," the guy shoots back straight-faced and sober. "He gave me this suit for my college graduation." "Oh" was all my client could manage at the time. What's your response?

- The new hire sitting around the lunch table at noon, who when a discussion breaks out about the occult and metaphysics, says, "People who run their lives according to astrology are so stupid, aren't they?" She was immediately informed that the company's owner, a demanding Leo, never made a corporate move without consulting the stars. She nearly slid out of her chair and under the table. What would you have done?

BUILDING UP TO NOTHING – TAKE ONE

EXT. UPPER MIDDLE CLASS HOME – PORTE COCHERE – LATE MORNING

CLOSE UP: Pale green, thick stucco façade of expensive home. Camera pans from large reed-glass double-door entry to wide shot of front entrance. Conversation well underway between homemaker and bidding architect

STANFORD
(Rigid. Features barely animating)

I'm interested in beating any other quote you get.

HOMEOWNER

I'll let you know

STANFORD
(Slightly cavalier)

Why don't you just have your husband call me so I can discuss
this with *him*.

Homemaker looks at Stanford with curious annoyance

STANFORD
I mean he is the decision maker, right?

HOMEOWNER
(Flatly)

I am the decision maker. I am single. I live here alone so I
am the *only* decision maker. **(Sarcastically)** Besides if I did
have a **(wraps finger tips around next word to frame air
quotes. Stretches pronunciation of it for more emphasis)**
"huuuuuussssband" we would make the decision together.

STANFORD
(Stumped)

I see …

SLOW DISSOLVE

HOOF IN MOUTH DISEASE

Wow? What age was this guy living in? Maybe he'd seen too much Andrew Dice Clay! It may sound outlandish that anyone in these modern times would be so chauvinistic or politically incorrect, but some people are, and conversations like this one happen all the time, and in the workplace, too.

This same architect came to me at the behest of a former student of mine who strongly suggested he see me. Actually, he really was a nice guy. Polite and courteous, he seemed like a perfect gentleman. But he was having trouble coming off that way to many of his would-be clients. I soon learned why.

Stanford (his first name) was quick to agree that he seemed to offend people both by his cool demeanor and also by his inappropriate dialogue. But, he confessed, he had absolutely no idea how to change his conversational style.

Like the previous students I discussed, Standford and I did a lot of role-playing. It was actually rather eye-opening for Stanford each time he took on the part of the homeowner. No one ever quite gets it until they walk around in the other guy's shoes!

He told me that after he said, "I see," she replied, "No, I don't think you do." She would find another architect with whom she felt she had a "good rapport," she finally told him. What did you say to that, I asked Stanford? He said he mumbled, "Well, okay then," as he made his leave. Oh boy, did we have work to do!

Poor Stanford, he knew no way of extracting the very large loafers crammed tightly in his metaphorical mouth. He even left the crime scene without as much as an apology.

I felt bad for Stanford because he didn't mean to offend the woman in any way. He explained with innocent eyes and soft voice that the woman had a huge house; that she was fairly young and so he couldn't imagine that she was making the mortgage payments by herself. He just assumed she had a husband and a second income. I attributed his poor dialogue with her to his upbringing, since he finally told me that he'd grown up in a family where his father had the final word on any financial decisions made in the home, in fact, oft times his father was the only one calling the shots.

Stanford was embarrassed to learn that his potential client

had started a clothing line in her late 20s, one that caught on immediately. As a result, she had made lots of money before the age of 30. She was now in her mid-thirties and wanting to make dramatic changes to her cliffhanging home in the posh Hollywood Hills.

Through a series of private coaching sessions, it became crystal clear to Stanford that he had stepped on the woman's toes when he made the suggestion that he speak to her husband. He also realized that an "I see" was not an effective or proper comeback on his part. Stanford confessed he had never been very good at rebounding in tense situations. He informed me that his knee-jerk response to a blunder was to find an exit line and vacate the scene. Sometimes he just left without a word.

MAKING AN EXIT

I was floored to learn about some of the other remarks that sent people like Stanford fleeing for the exit. As he began to trust me, realizing I truly wanted to help him and that I had no intention of judging him, he told me other stories. There was the time he said that he'd tried to buddy up to the gal at the fast-food place where he ducked in to get a quick sandwich as he went from one meeting to another. When she asked, "Want fries with that?" He laughed, pointed at her and said, "Are you kidding? I don't want to become a card-carrier in the big-butt club." With that I let out a quick "Oops." It may have been an okay thing to say to a bunch of guys in a locker room, but the young lady who waited on him, and the other three young ladies behind the counter, all had rather large rear ends. (This Stanford mentioned as a set up to telling me the story.) Stanford tried to show me the look on the girl's face from his inference. It was reminiscent of the signature McCauley Culkin expression in "Home Alone." He assured me he meant no harm, but it took Stanford some time to fully understand that putting his feet in his mouth was a serious issue with which he needed to deal. Though I never said it out loud, for fear of hurting his feelings, *Jaws of Life* is what often came to mind during my sessions with Stanford. It was going to take some pretty drastic measures to help him get his feet out of his mouth.

As the coach I had to keep my composure, though I've got to admit sometimes I wanted to burst out laughing at the absurdity of Stanford's blunders. For example, I darned near lost it the day Stanford told me that a client wanted a guest suite added to the design of existing architectural plans; it was for the client's mother-in-law who visited frequently. "If you would like," Stanford blurted, "I'll line it up right here, next to the dog house." This glib and cheeky remark, he assumed, would amuse his client. Not even. The client was stunned. *He* not only glared at Stanford, so did the client's wife who was watering plants a few feet away. Needless to say, Stanford was promptly let go.

VEERING TO THE CENTER

In Stanford's case, as in every case that comes to me, I prefer people step forward unless they have a consistent record of saying something tasteless, tacky or less than productive. Unfortunately, Stanford fell in the latter category.

I had to help Stanford get passed this problem. It would have to start by Stanford getting his mind in a different groove.

He wholeheartedly agreed.

Drive those thoughts down a more middle-of-the-road lane and err on the side of caution was my instruction to him. If you're not sure a thought should be expressed, don't speak it. Do your homework exercises to keep your thoughts fluid (I didn't want him going backwards and freezing up). Just discern which are appropriate to say and which are not. You can filter very quickly just like the improv player who has to make an instant choice. But, your job is to listen to that intuition, because it will be a lifesaver for you.

It sounded that when Stanford did speak he was quick and that was a plus. I didn't think speed was his number one problem. Rather, I think the issue for Stanford was going with impulses that were best kept at bay. So moving his mind to a different place is where I wanted him to initially go. If you're head operates in a more cautionary vein I told him, I feel certain your impulses will follow suit. I assured Stanford we would begin to tackle those times when he exited a scene with no parting line at all, but first things first!

"What's worse?" he asked, "Saying the wrong thing or saying nothing at all?" The wrong thing—always, I told him. I instructed Stanford to just step back for the time being until he could learn to step forward without doing so clumsily and to allow his thoughts to take on a conservative stance. "Pretend that you're talking to the President of the United States," I said, trying to give him what we call a *trick or secret* to make the mind shift to a different groove. "I'm sure you would be extremely careful with all your remarks to him." Stanford nodded a definitive yes to that.

How could Stanford begin to differentiate those thoughts that would offend those with whom he came in contact (especially potential clients) from those that were acceptable? I instructed him to consider the rights and wrongs of what he knew to be politically and socially correct. "If you're not sure of what is and what is not okay to express and to whom and when and where—bone up on your reading. Also watch informative television programs that address societal issues. Once you get a better grasp on *appropriateness* don't cross the line, Stanford," I said.

MOTHER MAY I?

As a way of getting through to Stanford, I asked him to think of how his mother might react to some of his remarks—the ones that got him into so much trouble. I learned that Stanford's mother had a great sense of humor along with loads of class. He let me know during several of our earlier sessions how impressed he was with her sense of diplomacy. "She has such a nice way of handling any situation, especially those where people are angry," he said. "Good, I told him, then observe her—use her as one of your communicator role models. Dwell on some of the most diplomatic things you recall her saying, especially as she was faced with awkward situations." He agreed to do so. "If you observe her long enough, you'll adopt her mental groove, too," I said. "For example, if you think of something to say and you know your mother would object, dismiss the thought and replace it with something else before you speak. Ask yourself, quickly, how your mother would react to that comment."

As a follow up to that idea, I suggested he hang out with

others he admired for their communication prowess in the diplomacy department—those at work and in his social circle—who had a knack for always saying the perfect thing. We pick up good habits from those we admire and those we are around. People tend to emulate what penetrates their psyche. (Think Pavlov's dog.)

I furthered Stanford's homework assignments by asking him to observe the not- so-appropriate types, too; the ones who constantly put their feet in their mouths. Just sit back and listen. It's the same thing I tell my actors. Watch other performers.

In one session, I asked Stanford to think about positive and negative communication traits he had picked up from the people around him. He did confide that his father had had a major influence on him and unlike Stanford's mother his father had been very abrupt and cold in his communication with others.

Watch, observe and study. Those were my final instructions to Stanford.

I'm now asking that you take on these same assignments. You can start by making a list of the people you know, or are around, who are verbal klutzes and another list that identifies the people who always respond with the perfect reply or comeback. If you're one who is apt to regularly blurt out the wrong thing, this assignment alone provides a superb glimpse of what future tact you may want to employ. Nothing like sitting on the sidelines and getting an objective view! It's similar to the assignment I give my improv comedy students. I tell them to go to an improv class in which they're not enrolled and to sit back and witness the dynamic among the students. They will gravitate toward the actors who are charming, playful and supportive of the other performers. They'll also take notice of the inappropriate types, the ones who are diving for the joke, who have little respect or consideration for the other players and who make tasteless remarks.

I talked Stanford into enrolling in one of my improv comedy courses as follow up to the Fast On Your Feet one-day session so he could be around quick-witted types weekly who acted on the rules of improv—in particular, the ones that emphasized diplomacy. I especially drilled the *Serve and Support* tenet into him. I couldn't think of a better assignment for Stanford, for he had been cloistered inside his own head. Working with others enabled him to redo scenes (conversations) that hadn't quite worked the first time and also closely observe his classmates. He made incredible progress. His mind began to work in a very socially constructive place and he was taking pride in his ability to ferret out the harmful verbal impulses from the productive ones.

If you can take such a class, do so. It's fun and such wonderful training to bolster overall communication technique. Doing drills repeatedly tends to reprogram the mind.

It took some time, but I finally got Stanford on track. Last I heard, he had signed a huge contract with a major Southern California developer to design the plans for several phases of high-end housing. He reported back that he was becoming truly successful at keeping his feet where they belonged—out of his mouth and planted firmly on the ground!

As I worked with Stanford, over the course of several months, I also gave him a list of homework tasks (in addition to the regular improv comedy class assignments); the same ones I'm now asking you to do, if you're one of those who tends to constantly put your feet in your mouth. Here they are:

- Observe others (but don't stare, you don't want to be labeled a stalker!).

- Take an improv comedy class or ask if you can audit one. See how the pros maneuver around tricky situations and manage to say the right thing. Who knows, you may end up with a new career—that of a featured player on "Saturday Night Live" or starring in your own sitcom.

- Seize the opportunity to save the moment when someone else says something that's out of line. That's right, jump in with a winning remark and save the day! This assignment is a big ego booster. I bet you'll have more than one opportunity a day to do this task.

- In order to reprogram your subconscious and make it more aware of getting your mind to stay down the "center," find a reminder symbol that you can keep nearby, one that you will look at constantly. A clue: Stanford carries around a shoehorn.

- Save the nasty comments (the inappropriate blurbs, the cutting remarks, the things you should never say out loud) for your drive home from work. Start talking and venting (if you're in the car alone) from office to home. Move your face around animatedly though so it will make it look like you're singing along with the radio. It's a great release! I have one student who does this on the way to a client's office—a person, she says, who is always throwing her for a curve which just infuriates her. She swears all the way to the meeting. By the time she sits down at the conference table she's feeling relieved and vindicated.

- If you're so inclined, keep a daily diary of those things you said that you shouldn't have said. Just playing back those awkward moments helps you steer away from repeating such counter-productive behavior in the future. If you're real ambitious, write down what you wished you *had* said, or think you could have said. Notice the difference between the two. If you want to cheat on this exercise (and you certainly can because I won't be there to watch you), ask one of your kids, a friend or your significant other what should have been said instead of the remark you made. Their feedback can be very enlightening.

- Don't be afraid to say "I'm sorry." It is one sure way to get your feet out of your mouth.

- If you want to get real inventive, go ahead and try to shove a real shoe in your mouth. Notice how hard it is to get in and out. It's a metaphorical lesson for not getting it stuck in there in the first place!

Know that there are no instances when inappropriate remarks can work to your benefit. What you want is to connect with people and establish rapport, always, period. In business, like in our personal lives, it's all about relationships. Relationships are built on camaraderie and respect. When we say the wrong thing it can repel the very people we're trying to engage. So my request is this: If you tend to put your foot in your mouth like Stanford, step back for a time until you learn to step gracefully forward. And don't forget to practice all your assignments more than once. Repetition is wonderful conditioning of those mental muscles and also a terrific way to reprogram your mental response mechanism.

Let's move on now to a discussion of how to stay firm and grounded, especially in the midst of difficult people—the ones that typically make you freeze in your tracks.

"The Creole Convertible is ... is ...could somebody ... please ... turn TelePrompter back on ...please?"

Chapter Seven

HEAD OVER HEELS:
Standing Firm And Grounded

RIGHT ME UP – TAKE ONE

INT. MANPOWER TRUCKING, INC.—V.P. OF HR
OFFICE – RIGHT AFTER LUNCH

FADE IN SLOWLY

VOICE OVER
Sharon feels like she's fending off a mortar attack. Never expected her six-month performance review to resemble a trial at Nuremberg or the Spanish Inquisition. Her natural response to the veiled insults coming at her is to duck, dive ... hot-foot-it to the doorway.

Personality clashes, common in Sharon's department. Everyone's a manager with shared responsibility (and shared "billing"). Squabbles are common. Sharon's refusal to get involved in office politics is suddenly to her disadvantage. Seems she's fast becoming the department's scapegoat.

Female commando in HR is putting it to her:

HR DIRECTOR
(Haughty)

I'd like to think everyone in our region is a team player, Sharon.

SHARON
(Silence)

HR DIRECTOR
(Imperious)

I have to write you up for not participating in the roundtable on the revamp of the manager's manual.

SHARON
(Wants to explain. Unsure of how to coin a viable response. Sharon's lips part. Tries to speak, but no go)

HR DIRCTOR
(Officious)

I won't name names, because you know I don't do that. **(Pontificating)** But two others very close to you have let me know that when it comes to group discussions, you simply clam up. Let me put it another way, you refuse to contribute.

SHARON
(Can take no more)

With all due respect, Ms. Canfield, there seems to be a dysfunctional dynamic among the group. Rather than get involved in what I consider petty struggles over whose suggestions will prevail, I find it much more productive to sit on the sidelines. I have, however, offe ...

CANFIELD
(Cuts her off)

Sorry, Sharon, that leaves me no choice but to add that to the report. The top brass made it very clear that everyone would participate no matter how differing the team's points of view.

FREEZE FRAME

V.O.

There was so much Sharon wanted to say, but her internal frustration—blocked her from adequately formulating, much less articulating, her thoughts. Why does this always happen, she thought? Why do my thoughts get murky and muddled when someone gets in my face (pause) and when I know full well what it is I want to communicate?

FADE OUT

I've been in Sharon's shoes. How about you? When the pressure is greatest during a confrontational situation like this one, many of us are overcome with fury, fear or frustration which precludes us from calmly and succinctly spitting out what we (unfortunately) think to say moments or hours later.

I don't know about you, but after a confrontational bout (one in which I've been unable to rebound with immediate responses) it causes me to wake up in the middle of the night. Rather than counting sheep, I try to get myself back to sleep by counting the many choices of what it is I *wished* I had said. Forget arriving at one perfect remark, I come up with several. Then I begin to inject each of them in the pivotal part of the scene—first reciting my parts, then theirs, often until the sun comes up!.

After addressing the smorgasbord of options of all the things I might have said, methodically trying to match them up against the things said to me, I lament my failure for having had no personally satisfying reply at all. What hell!

DAY TRIPPIN'

Maybe your mind is dancing around in the dark and not

just at night, but perhaps you're carrying such thoughts into the following day, having them distract you from important business at hand. After a sleep-deprived night, you may find yourself missing important cues in a meeting or sales call (like having to ask the person's name three or four times because you just can't concentrate), or plunging over the edge behaviorally as you find yourself overindulging in one thing or another. That one thing could be drinking, eating junk food, shopping …. I had one female student who couldn't look me in the eye when she finally whispered that she had taken to eating an entire box of Twinkies in the middle of the night each time her hostile boss chastised her. (She had a dozen plus Ho-Ho's the night he berated her for leaving the lid open on the copier earlier that morning!) After several months on the job she had gained a substantial amount of weight. Last I heard, she was doing marvelously well using her added Fast tools (she didn't want to quit her job because she loved it too much) and holding true to Jenny Craig.

If you at all resemble me or the young lady I just mentioned, this chapter will be most helpful to you. I've added a few tricks to the basic Fast tool belt to keep you more in the game when those irritating or grueling confrontations not only sweep you off your feet (your Center), but virtually consume you.

I tell my students that when the playback of difficult communication situations reaches the point where it affects their appetite, forces them to lose sleep (or sleep too much), causes them to over-do (or under-do), or puts a dent in their otherwise sunny disposition, it's time to add some more Fast remedies to their Fast starter kit.

HUNKERING DOWN

It was through my own travails and those of my students that I began to ruminate over what sort of added concoction I needed to dream up as an adjunct to the Fast formula—extra tactics that would help them when the Big Confrontation took place.

My first task was that of compiling data from all my one-on-one conferences with students—those in particular who had also lain awake in bed at night and those who had allowed themselves to remain at the affect of the kind of self-torture that only comes from "I shoulda-coulda said."

I couldn't believe some of the instances people shared with me. Two of my favorites: the guy whose female boss kicked his briefcase across the conference room in a fit of rage telling him he would be next, and the female whose immediate supervisor blamed her lipstick color for the company's contract loss in front of the entire team of her male counterparts. Harassment you might say? Cause for lawsuits? Maybe, but that's not the point. That's for each of them to decide. My job was more immediate: I needed to help these people and others like them to square off conversationally in the face of such horrifying moments—help them find appropriate ways to stand firm and grounded while speaking up unflinchingly.

Next, I began to play with different ideas of what combo platter I might brew up as an addendum to what I already had in place. Naturally, I realized the Fast formula all by itself just wasn't going to be enough. Sure, the formula was going to keep these students from being without a loss for words in many tense situations, but what about those times when the Big Heckler showed up? This, it seemed, required a little something extra.

While my students, in general, always admitted that they had had their share of moments when they were tongue-tied, thus experiencing some discomfort and/or regret, there was a marked distinction between *that* group, the ordinary "Want-to-be-Fast On Your Feeters" and the secondary group: those who were virtually crushed by verbal uppercuts and who suffered angst from the inability to throw a counter-punch. These were the folks who were not only taking it home from the office with them and agonizing over it for a time, they were the ones tossing and turning during the middle of the night.

I invited all those who fell into this category to join me for further exploration and study. When I met with them, this latter group reported in that they were using the *Think-Fast Formula* and plenty of the Fast exercises I'd recommended, but it wasn't quite enough for them when it came time to deal with confrontations. No question then, I had to find that something else that I could meld into the Fast mix.

ON THEIR TOES

After the student interviews, note gathering, compiling the data, digesting it and sifting through some possibilities, I got to thinking: Perhaps I ought to implement a Special Forces-type of improv training; a more intense mental boot camp just for them. So I augmented the existing curriculum with a tag-on addendum—one that would make this group strong and steady (and well-rested) no matter what the situation, no matter who the *enemy*.

I needed this follow-up lesson plan to also lay out ways for this group of students to find methods to let go of a situation soon after it was over.

Sleep is an important part of the plan, I told them as I interviewed each one after they had graduated the Fast 101 class and before passing them onto the Fast Lab. If you're not getting the rest your physical system needs, you're far more likely to crumble in the face of your adversaries. Most of us are in a very vulnerable state when overly tired.

For the sleepless, it had become a vicious cycle I learned during my investigation. Those I'd interviewed confided that they were unable to respond during confrontations when faced with the same difficult people repeatedly because they couldn't gather their thoughts well enough. This they attributed to exhaustion, so each time they came into verbal contact with these folks, the problem compounded itself.

Part of my assignment then was to help this group of tormented communicators discard the negative communication experience so they could conk out at night and stay that way until alarm time, enabling them to go to work the following day where they would be firmly on their toes!

This same group also revealed that when stuck in a state of frustration or anger, many found themselves skidding into some form of nonproductive behavior—either new bad habits they'd acquired, or overdoing destructive old ones. It was probably the sweet, young tearful female administrative assistant who told me she was throwing on a pair of jeans and driving half-way across town to play blackjack at a card club in the middle of the night that gave me the extra resolve I needed to get a plan in tow. With a slight fist-pound on my desk's top, I firmly decided that this adjunct training had to be so stringent and so grueling that the real circumstances each student might encounter with a confrontational type would be a piece of cake to them. Yep, Special Forces training, that was the way to go!

ONE STEP AT A TIME

After getting my lesson plan in order, I took my first group of eager students, sat them down and provided some introductory remarks. I told them that they would learn to stay solidly planted no matter how much the other guy (s) wanted or tried to topple them, and I wanted them to be open to the idea that it was indeed possible. My goal for each of them was to remain steadfast. I didn't want them to so much as tremble (even inwardly) at the site of the difficult person. And when it came time for conversation with such people, I wanted each of them to operate from a quick, ready and *steady* mind. Most important of all, I told them, I didn't want any of them reliving the situation long after it was over. My ultimate goal was for each of them to be able to release the event—leave it behind them by dumping it into a mental trashcan. I didn't want the after-affects of any communication situation controlling them in any way or setting them up for some kind of no-esteem roller coaster either, as they moved forward dealing with other similar difficult types.

Yes, I was on a mission!

Since all were desperate for a remedy and they knew I really cared deeply about them, they willingly bought into my Fast-lab-stay-after-school recruitment program. Each enlisted in the advanced extra Fast day of tutoring. Not one dropped out.

SHAKE YOUR GROOVE THING

I'm big on understanding. With that in mind, Step #1 in my initial lesson in the Special Forces boot camp training began with an analysis of what it was that caused people to lose it when confronted. Subsequently, I explained, I would get each of them to come to grips with what "it" was for each of them.

So, I began to dig.

After enough observation of Sharon's and the others' situations, and after analyzing what exactly happens when people hurl offensive, hurtful or abusive remarks anyone's way, I came to realize that often humiliation is at the core of the problem. It's an emotion that causes most of us to slam on the mental brakes. I discussed this to some extent in Chapter Two, when I covered Inhibition (you may want to review the *caring-too-much* principle).

A loss of concentration accompanies humiliation (like the kind that Sharon had experienced) disables us, for how can anyone snatch and then grab onto a viable response (floating across our minds like a news crawl), and speak it, when we are so distracted by shame. Being put down or denigrated generally causes each of us to slip out of our natural groove. The keyword here is groove. Groove is vital to handling confrontation.

What am I referring to when I say groove?

I'm talking about verbal rhythm, one's natural flow. We all have a certain rhythm. We move and react rhythmically when we're engaged in physical activities. Not only dancing or playing sports, but when brushing our teeth, shaking the popcorn over the stove, flipping the remote control or even vacuuming. Our groove is something we don't even think about when we're comfortable. It's just there. We notice our own trademark groove with the cadence of our walk and how we phrase our sentences, where we pause and hold. This is most evident when telling stories or recounting experiences to those with whom we are most comfortable. That groove screeches to a halt when we have been shocked or surprised by a remark we didn't see coming. Once off kilter, we have no flow. No flow, no verbal rhythm. You can only have rhythm when a cadence repeats itself. Yes, tempo is a critical component to keeping a conversation moving along.

It's the dead air that takes us down every time.

One thing I came to realize during my initial investigation of looking at Sharon's and her groups' very serious problem is that they had all fallen out of their natural groove in the presence of their confronter. So getting familiar with their groove thing was Step #2: The second kick-off point. Think about it. When your groove is disturbed (your natural rhythm flow) it's going to affect everything from speech to sleep

Lack of groove also affects your habits. It can promote the good ones and exacerbate the bad ones. Momentum and rhythm are interrelated.

So for starters, our group class assignment included a series of exercises that forced each student to reacquaint him or herself with their groove thing.

We made short speeches about hobbies and likes and dislikes, getting in touch with our sense of phrasing as we spoke.

We made up poems.

We dribbled a basketball.

We danced.

We hopped.

We snapped our fingers.

When we had finished this series of assignments, each person was far more aware of what felt rhythmically natural to them and what did not.

You can do the same. Put the book down for a minute and get up and walk back and forth across the room. Note the tempo of your steps.

Dance. Become aware of how you move to the music.

Snap your fingers. See how precise the snapping is between intervals of silence.

Talk. Call a friend and try to note the personal cadence of your own dialogue. Pay attention to how effortlessly your dialogue flows when you're in a comfortable groove.

Doing each of these assignments may seem rather strange at first, but I promise, each is designed to increase mental flow and also to make you aware of what happens when you lack groove. Groove can be your best friend when you want to come back with a suitable response—no matter how hostile or obdurate the other person is on her end of the conversation. If your groove is undisturbed, it will keep the verbal integrity in tact.

Toning your rhythm muscles (mentally) serves to keep you movin' and groovin' no matter what goes down conversationally. With enough practice you will become more aware of your groove thing and how it fits in with keeping your composure when facing confrontations! So, get going! Move in *time*.

My improv players spend weeks doing nothing but timing exercises. They are given, for instance, the first line of a newly-made-up poem. They are required to recite the first line and without *any* hesitation, continue to spout off the rest of the poem in a definitive rhythm as though it was written and they were reciting it from memory. They know that the slightest hesitation will break their stride and dismantle their groove. Once the groove is gone, it is almost impossible to get it back. Want to know what causes them to hesitate? Same thing that causes you to hesitate in the presence of a confronter: A jolt of inhibition!

STOPPING DEAD IN YOUR TRACKS

After this group and I completed all our *groove* tasks (we danced the night away, by the way, as we boogied to a lot of Earth Wind and Fire), we began Step #3: Explore the issue of what goes on in the mind (without getting too psychological) of one who is faced with a hostile individual or one that makes us feel diminished or disenfranchised.

"Easy to go into a tailspin of horror," I quipped. They agreed. "Hard to pull out of such a mental dive, yes?" They agreed with that as well. "We play dead," one shy student blurted (his breakthrough came when he taught us the 70's dance craze, the Mashed Potato, moments earlier). Many of us do play dead as a means to avoid the trauma. We check out. We shut down. We're not quite conscious. If we are still semi-conscious, our minds begin to race with fragmented thoughts like "Help me!" "Now what do I do?" "Get me out of here! "It's like the animal that is hit by a car; one that is often terribly injured, but manages to stagger to the side of the road. Opting for safety and laying quiet is very often all most of us can do at a time like that. In the midst of such trauma no one feels much like talking.

I'm told the U.S. Army's Special Forces trooper never succumbs to the circumstances placed before him, nor does he run the other way. He plows through the hit. He is trained to *lock down* quickly and solidly perform, especially in the face of adversity no matter how severe. "React like the Special Forces type," I told Sharon and the others I was coaching in this *special* unit. The trooper never looses his groove. Keeping it is ingrained in him; the very reason why he reacts and responds, without any hesitation while under great duress.

Think about it!

You, too, can train like the trooper. With rigorous *mental* exercises that *over-prepare* your mental faculties to do the opposite of freezing up (in addition to those we already covered in the Four-Step, like the rhythm exercises and the added ones I just mentioned) you can remain unflappable, I don't care how hostile, mean, insensitive or offensive the other person becomes.

A KICK IN THE STANCE

Once we analyzed what stopped us in our tracks (Step #1), then got in touch with finding our groove (Step #2) and understood what happens to our concentration level under great mental stress (Step #3), it was time to get into the heavy stuff. Step #4: Putting each student in grave danger: A mock face-to-face verbal combat situation with a difficult person.

I arranged for this assignment to be conducted during private one-on-one sessions.

I got squarely in each person's face and began by telling them we were going to have a conversation about a work-related issue with a difficult person (they identified who that was ahead of time on a questionnaire). The conflict or experience with that person served as the centerpiece for our dialogue. I warned them that the things I was going to say might seem harsh and sometimes cruel, but if they could maintain their cool in the midst of such grilling attacks, and speak up appropriately, they could probably handle anyone in the real-world workplace with those who drove them up a wall. It was risky, yes, but I made sure each Ranger was up to the task by thoroughly explaining ahead of time how the mock scene would be conducted. They were game. I played the Bad Guy and began firing off shots.

Sharon was my first inductee. We revisited her scene with the HR Director. I played the latter part (it was kind of fun!).

"You didn't participate because you're dumb," I barked. When she tried to speak, I said, "Oh, you think you have something of value to contribute now? Well, it's just too late! Don't say a word," I warned.

Sharon began to get flushed.

"Oh," I continued snidely with a mock tone in my voice,

"That upset you? Well, that's just too dammed bad, isn't it?"

Sharon just sat there near tears as I overdid my role in the scenario. I continued to pummel her; keeping her off guard with more offensive jabs. I made some of them personal. "I hate your shoes. They're stupid, like you."

She gasped. She was so taken aback she couldn't speak.

Shocking perhaps to even think I would do such a thing, but it worked. After a few more rounds she finally set aside her humiliation and got a little mad. A few rounds after that she began to speak up, lobbing remarks back at me. When I told her I thought she probably had an I.Q. of 60, she said between clenched jaws, "That is unacceptable. How could you possibly say such a thing like that to *anyone*? You should be ashamed."

"You go, girl!" I finally said as I signaled that the exercise was over. Getting Sharon to speak up under such a horrendous verbal attack was what I had hoped for as an *initial* breakthrough, a very critical step. I didn't want her to sit paralyzed from trauma, crumbling under a recurring wave of humiliation. Finally, she hadn't and I was proud of her.

"I never want you at a loss for words, Sharon. Ever," I told her. "I want you to feel comfortable and free to speak up—to say the things that are appropriate and in defense of your position, and to say them without anger and more with authority and grace.

The fact that Sharon had ultimately kept her dignity and didn't respond with *like* remarks, despite my machine-gun insults, showed me that she had the ability to maintain both her grasp and her cool. I warned her that I didn't want her to get to the point where she was so angry that she was speaking between clenched teeth. I wanted her to speak firmly, but kindly, responding immediately to the confronting remark.

She had become somewhat angry as she worked up to being able to speak that day, but that was perfectly okay during that session. Her slight outburst moved her past the frozen tongue stage. That's all I expected. Later she could learn to gather herself and not show disgust or anger.

Hooray for Sharon! She at least had conquered her debilitating fear, was able to concentrate and stay in her groove. From that point, I knew she had an excellent chance of saving herself from sleepless nights and demoralizing regret. I knew training her to come up with *appropriate* responses on the dime would become easier for her.

"Great, we got past that hurdle," I smiled. She impulsively hugged me!

Each of the other students, during similar sessions, took their place on the hot seat. I threw in twists now and again to keep them off guard so as to try and trip them up. Some I did; others I didn't. All were exhausted (me too!) when we finished.

BACKING UP

Backtracking a bit: Step #1 in Sharon's case, as well as the others, was to get them to analyze what happens when they are instantly humiliated by another person. In other words, what happens to induce the complete halt of the mental process? Again, as the one student so articulately pointed out with Step #3, we play dead.

Next, if you recall, we looked at Step #2: Groove. When the brain freezes, as it attempts to assimilate shame and embarrassment, it loses its natural flow from thought to spoken words. It's hard to stay in the conversational flow when groove goes out the window.

By holding fast to Step #2—staying true to your groove thing, it is far easier to engage the enemy in equal measure. In terms of Step #3, I'll tell you what I told my "stay-afters": Focus on self-power. When the pressure is on, turn up your own heat as you hunker down. When you've been kicked, don't fall to your knees. Stand taller and stronger!. Keep your game mind on.

Steps # 1, 2 and 3 make sense, but how do you master them? It comes as a result of thickening your concentration level so for a refresher, go back to Chapter Three and do your concentration exercises. The repetitive drills will reinforce your ability to stay in the moment with a firm grip no matter what unexpected incident befalls you.

Revisit Chapter Two and redo some of your assignments for lessening your inhibitions. Remember, humiliation creates inhibition and inhibition can stop you in your mental tracks, every time you're faced with it.

Now, go back through the book and reread many of the discussions about the parallels between you and the improv player and what happens to improv players when under intense pressure. That alone will remind you how much you have in common with them.

One thing I didn't cover yet is what improv comedy players do when they are confronted or harassed. When improv players are faced with a confrontational crisis that could easily ruffle their composure (let's say an audience member heckles, or harasses them on stage or demeans them), rather than becoming meek and shrinking deep within from embarrassment, they muster up an energy surge that powers them right past that tendency to hesitate. Improv players' resolve, or what they term *commitment*, enables them to plow right through the overwhelming remark and circumvent the tendency to become inhibited. Free and steady, they rely on their mental faculties to come forth with an appropriate response—be it to the out-of-line audience member or the other players with whom they are interacting.

I also covered energy in Chapter Three and I suggest you repeat those exercises, practicing them regularly just as improv comedy players do. Don't forget what I pointed out in that chapter: Instead of imploding their energy and playing dead to protect their feelings or mitigate their discomfort, improv players mentally and verbally floor it. They are trained like the Special Forces Trooper. Rather than retreating, they advance and face the enemy head-on. Nothing dismantles the Improv Comedy Trooper's concentration, or their groove or commitment to stay the course!

Remember this: In the Fast Game there is no pulling back. If you get scared, over-commit. Get more active. If you get intimidated, get courageous. Sound strange or impossible? It's not at all. What it comes down to is training. Training and repetition reconditions and reprograms the mind. So when you get the urge to curl up in a mental ball and retreat, do the opposite. Throw yourself out there. Think about the concept of *fight or flight*. Resolve not to flee, instead fight, but in a non-combative, powerfully constructive way. Your goal is to perform well verbally under the direst of circumstances.

THE FOURTH POSITION

Step #5 in the Fast Special Forces Training Manual has to do with preparation. Sound contradictory to the overall "improv" concept? It's not.

Though I realize I have preached constantly to you about staying in the moment and going with the flow, this added tool will help you prepare for staying in the game by *working out* ahead of time, much like the Special Forces Trooper swings on ropes through trees for conditioning purposes. Though you have prepared—gotten strong and ready mentally just like the Trooper does physically—you still need to rely on your improv ability and that's what this book is all about in many ways: getting in superb shape in order to perform as an excellent improv player!

I asked Sharon and her special-trooper group, and I'm asking you, too, to add this new tool to your Fast tool belt. It's an exercise actually, and once comfortable fiddling with it, you may choose to rely on it heavily as a formidable warm-up device before you meet with Mr. or Ms. Difficult. ExecuProv calls it the Fast Track, My Stance game.

Step #5 is for those instances when you know ahead of time that your pending encounter may be a challenging one. Yes, this is the one time I tell my students to go ahead and anticipate what a difficult person may say *beforehand* and begin to rehearse how they *might* handle the scene before it takes place. For example, in Sharon's case, she knew that her supervisor was going to challenge her on her lack of input during the round table meetings. She was very clear on the meeting's one agenda item. If she could have anticipated certain eventualities of that conversation that may have come up during that meeting, and had the opportunity to practice several approaches to potential attacks or questions put to her, she might have been able to stay in her groove rather than clamming up and shutting down.

I wasn't asking Sharon, nor am I asking you, to preplan your *dialogue*, but rather I'm recommending that you adopt a *strategy*; consider the position you will take if you know a confrontation is imminent. In Sharon's case, she could have pondered whether to point out the shortcomings in having the entire team make a collective decision on the management manual, or suggest one person be in charge of it, or, when confronted, ask the HR Director to attend a meeting in order to see how nonproductive one actually was. With the My Stance game she could have seized the opportunity to think about how she might handle the situation once confronted.

This preplanning exercise I'm recommending is very similar to the theory behind the method political candidates use to train for debates. They may not know the questions ahead of time, only the general categories. In the now-vogue town hall debate setting, for instance, most candidates have no idea what the exact queries will be, only the general topic on which they will be asked to comment. They spend hours getting their thoughts, ideas, and most importantly, their platforms together in order to prepare for a question on a topic they know will be covered. When the question is posed to them, they are expected to respond without skipping a beat. A huge part of their preparation is deciding what their position will be on a matter ahead of time.

By the way, this My Stance game might help you alleviate the remorse that often comes *after* the encounter when you run through all the things you wanted or wished you *had* said. So why not reverse the process and take some of that mental energy and decide ahead of time what your overall *strategy* will be. This type of preparation is the perfect way to tune up for the real thing because you will be ready to state your case even if you don't know what will be said during the confrontation. (It's also great for creativity and toning your mental muscles.) If you're going to lay awake at night, I would rather you do it *before* the encounter takes place. Coming to grips with your stance and gearing up to present it the following day often stimulates an adrenaline flow — that extra boost you may need to stay strong as the confrontation unfolds. Think: Conviction!

I've tried out the My Stance game on Sharon and a number of others. They have all said the same thing: The actual meeting was not nearly as difficult as they imagined it might be since they had prepared a strategy ahead of time to take to the battlefield.

I want you to do the same.

Pinpoint what your position will be so you will be better prepared as those questions or verbal attacks come flying at you.

Rehearse the impending scene if it makes you feel better. Performing it a dozen or so ways and try out more than one strategy if you like, but use all your improv tools and imagination in the process, of course. An added benefit of doing this activity, in addition to having your mind in a definitive place, is that you will have taken time to fully process your ideas and feelings, as well as analyze the situation that lies ahead. Some therapists might label this over-thinking, but I think it's one more way to suit up for the Big Game. When I'm nervous or uneasy about a pending encounter and have a general idea about the nature of the confrontation about to take place, I generally run my strategy or approach the *day* before (not at night when I need my eight hours). Sometimes I cheat and come up with potential remarks I might make in response to what I think may be said. I've learned over time, as I stated earlier in the book, that the conversations rarely go the way I think they will. Still, for me and others like me who dread the confrontational situation, some anticipation can prove to be invaluable as the attack gets underway. Doing this exercise, my students tell me, fires them up so that they are at the ready to bolt out the verbal gate with less fear and a strong position against that of the antagonist. If you're a controlling type, the My Stance game is the exercise for you!

What also appeals to me about this exercise is that it has a way of forcing you to remain in your Think-Fast Groove; the place where all the right answers come from! Doing this drill will stimulate a reprogramming of sorts and assist you in taking the next step: Quickly nabbing one of those "armed answers" when the confrontation actually gets underway. Think of yourself as the Special Forces Trooper and your decided-upon strategy as gear strapped around your mental waistband.

But wait a minute, you might be thinking, if my task is to train like the improv comedy player, isn't Step #5 a violation of the improv comedy player's credo: To fly by the seat of their pants? No, it isn't. Let me explain why. When improv comedy players ready themselves for the evening's performance *they practice the premises of the scenes they know will be in the show.* And, as they do this preparation, they play artfully with their predetermined strategy for taking on an improv piece. For instance, we might choose to work on the political debate skit. The premise for this scene is that two actors will portray political candidates who begin arguing over a ridiculous topic. One night the audience suggested they debate over Tapioca pudding. One was for it, the other against it. Each actor had already decided the strategy he would employ with each political candidate character. One decided to be a bombastic know-it-all while the other picked a strategy of talking in circles, never making any sense whatsoever, despite how knowledgeable he tried to come across. It was the *strategies* (the points of view on how they would approach those characters and the mechanics of the debate piece itself) that they emphasized during rehearsal, rather than the setup from the audience which they would not know until that evening during the show.

Now, when the improv actors engage in the My Stance exercise, they can't avoid getting caught up in the actual dialogue in the scene for they have to practice with some fodder. But the workout is to help them get their individual strategies in tow.

In another improv piece, "The Auditions" (one of my favorites to watch!), the audience members become talent scouts and we ask them to write down ridiculous talents for each of the players who will take to the stage and profess to be exceptional at them. The actors are seated, then they stand one at a time when called upon, grab a written suggestion out of a hat, read it quickly and launch into acting it out (with great confidence, I might add). While rehearsing this piece, I might ask one player to sing "Yankee Doodle Dandy" backwards, and another to recite the Gettysburg address, skipping every other word. (I'll never forget the night one of our 14-year old killer improv players was asked to sing the "Hokey Pokey" in Vietnamese, or the night a seasoned improv player sat in with my Crazies troupe and was asked to play a harmonica with her derriere and perform the Dylan favorite: "Blowin' in the Wind" and believe it or not, she performed this request in good taste and very cleverly, too).

After the actors act out the special talent, they field random questions from the audience. Once again, during the rehearsal their preparation is more focused on the nature of the piece and their stance toward it or the character they're playing, rather than the questions or challenges that will be put before them. Rehearsal time enables them to get the strategy down which in turns prepares them well for whatever they are actually confronted with during the show.

The My Stance exercise warm-ups serve to do something else for the improv team: These drills help them put into play the other Steps in this added Fast Formula. What the improv player does is much like what you are doing with some improv-type advance planning: Gearing up to power through any conversational obstacle, irrespective of how weird or demanding the scene gets. You're also accustoming yourself to the possibility you may need to slide into another's energy field readily without having to work at doing so (getting into *their* groove, fast).

Yes, here we go with *groove* again! Perhaps you've seen improv players switch from working with one cast member to another rapidly, or even with a person plucked from the audience. There is no shifting around until they are comfortably implanted into the other's groove, they just join up with that groove, and begin to dialogue compatibly. With enough practice doing Step #5, you'll soon do the same. Here's some My Stance homework to get you going:

1. List the name or names of the person (s) with whom you are likely to have a confrontation:

    _____

    _____

    _____

    Example:
    Joan Blake, president of Box-it Packing, my company's largest client.

2. What types of confrontation (s) have you experienced with this person (s)?

    _____

    _____

    _____

    Example:
    Last week Joan Blake told me off on a conference call with my boss on the line.

3. Write down what was said:

    _____

    _____

    _____

Example:
"You made a mistake on last month's billing. That's twice now. I'm really tired of your mathematical errors. You are *so* inept!"

4. Write down your response:

    _____

    _____

    _____

Example:
I said nothing, I just stammered for a few minutes and my boss took over apologizing for my error and for the company.

5. For drill, go ahead and write down at least four choices of what you wished you had said:

    _____

    _____

    _____

    _____

Example:
a. (Kindly) First, I'm very sorry. Please accept my apology.
b. (Kindly, but firmly) I understand your frustration and I am truly sorry, but I need to ask that you not refer to me as inept.
c. (Confidently) We all make mistakes, yet talking to me abusively—with all due respect—will not make things better. I am happy to redo the billing to your satisfaction.
d. (Somewhat humorously) Two errors don't make a person inept. It makes her human!
e. (If you want to meet her on her turf) I am truly sorry, but let me just say, I would much rather agonize over

having made two mathematical errors than to ever regret having made the mistake of talking to anyone in such a deprecating manner, as you just have to me.

6. Write down any future encounters you anticipate having with this person

_____

_____

_____

Example:
I have a standing weekly conference call to go over all billings with Joan Blake.

7. Potential situations in which I may find myself in a bind with Ms. Blake:

_____

_____

_____

Examples:
a. She always hassles me about extra charges.
b. She blows up when she doesn't understand a line item.
c. Her tendency is to say she asked for something specific in the report that she really did not ask for.

Now play the My Stance game with assignment #6. Make up at least two strategies for this student, ones you might employ with each scenario:

_____

_____

_____

Examples:
a. I will approach the situation with sincerity and apologeticallyno matter how the dialogue plays out.
b. My strategy will be to let her know in no uncertain terms,immediately or during the course of the conversation, that *her* approach to reprimanding me is not acceptable.

180

Had the person conversing with Ms. Blake done the My Stance exercise before the confrontation took place (the one she knew was pending) she may have been ready to choose between some of the answers typically thought of afterwards, like the ones I listed in Drill #5.

After completing the My Stance assignment above, lay out one of your own and provide comments you think might be appropriate; ones that demonstrate you are holding your own. I believe with enough rehearsal, you'll gain confidence in terms of spewing out a host of potential responses that *back up your strategy,* ones that just might fit the bill when you're actually on the spot. If you're at a loss with what to write down while doing this portion of the homework, ask a friend or loved one to help. Sometimes we can't think outside our box. Collaborating is always a great idea if you're writing a script. This assignment is like writing a sketch or a screenplay. Have some fun because you're the author!

Start this task by writing down the confrontation (it's what we call a *conflict* in improv parlance). Next, decide on how you will approach the conflict. Now play it out. Go ahead and write the presupposed dialogue and feel free to jot down several options that line up nicely with your strategy.

While doing this, don't forget to go with your Instincts, Impulses and Intuition. It's one more way to strengthen those spontaneity muscles of yours.

PUT YOUR FEET UP

In addition to understanding your groove, your need for concentration, and the push for energy and resolve (as well as your practice sessions playing the My Stance game) Step # 6 is a tool my students tell me is a real lifesaver! This step is also another terrific trick in preparing to take on the antagonist at the exact moment in time when he or she is challenging or harassing you.

This final step requires that you **detach** from the trauma of the situation as you're in the midst of it.

That may sound like a contradiction in terms, but it's not, really. When I say detach, I mean to have the strength and presence to keep a professional distance from your emotions—the ones that cause you to relinquish your natural groove and play dead. These are the same emotions that distract you from the present and escalate the remorse in you to such a feverish pitch that you can't sleep at night or you drown your frustration in Five-Card Stud or Twinkies.

Sounds reasonable, but how can you possibly detach? Like the improv player you learn to be totally immersed in the moment with attention to detail and *not yourself.* That enables you to become successful in separating your self from the actual trauma as it's going down. Though I have had many years of practice, I find that I slip comfortably away from the scene—create enough distance between how I am being made to feel and how I would respond to such feelings if I were just a fly on the wall—that I remain anchored, steady and tactically in the game. By stepping back, I find I can also remain objective about the circumstances at hand. Objectivity is a great ally in getting me through such rough situations. I've gone so far as to pretend it's someone else in my body or mind at the moment of great stress (it's a flip-the-switch thing) and I'm just sitting on the sidelines coaching myself through it. This allows me to take a back seat emotionally (so the jabs are not so painful) and pull back to assess the enemy. As such, I'm much quicker to access the appropriate strategy—as well as the right verbal response.

Detaching from the enemy is not all that different from how the Special Forces Trooper functions during combat. These soldiers do not have the luxury of wallowing in their fear at *that* moment or taking the situation personally. They must engage the enemy while they loftily disengage from all attachment to it. This may sound complex or impossible, but it can be done.

Here's how I approached this tactic with Sharon. I told her I wanted her to imagine she was her best friend (Marty was her name) and that she, as Marty, was witnessing Sharon getting a grilling from the HR Monster. Now, as Marty, she was once removed from the trauma and began to think and react the way she would if she were Marty, sideline-coaching Sharon. The improv player does the same thing under grave pressure. He or she steps back and detaches from the sheer horror of having to execute the perfect dialogue to fit the moment in the scene when the pressure becomes too severe. Sure it takes a lot of practice for improv comedy players to be able to do this so instantaneously, but they practice and they work out until it is ingrained in them. Only in this state can they remain loose and objective enough to react and respond instantly and appropriately. So they are doing a dual task: They are staying committed, powering through the bad energy, and detaching from the fright of it, simultaneously.

Sadly, what most people do is they become so self-consumed and so *self* conscious that all they can think about is how they *feel* in response to the attack. Typically, they withdraw.

If this is happening to you, I want you to pay particular attention to the homework tasks below because I know they will be a big help to you.

STEPPING UP TO THE PLATE

Detaching is an advanced Fast technique that will take time to master, but the homework for this Step #6 is fun.

- Put yourself in an uncomfortable situation with a coworker or colleague, and as you're conversing with them, take a few minutes during your conversation to pretend you're someone else and respond as that someone might respond. What I want you to grasp, even if it's momentary at first, is the sensation that you are not you at all, but someone else who you tend to rely upon—that someone who always seems to say the right thing at the right time. In our follow-up discussion with the entire Special forces class, my students were asked to share-and-tell of at least one instance when they detached from themselves in conversation. It didn't have to be a confrontational situation, but preferably a tense one. One student, debating with a coworker over what direction their new product rollout strategy should take, told me he pretended he was not himself but Martin Luther King. Another said he imagined Vince Lombardi was coaching him from the sidelines as he sparred over the best way he and his partner could approach their PowerPoint presentation. During a discussion over pop tarts versus toast, one woman chose to become her mother, giving her that feel of extraordinary authority. And another young lady, embroiled in a heated exchange with the guy in the cubicle next to her over the Red Sox and the Yankees, told me she envisioned herself floating above the desk looking down on the two of them. One of my 40-year-old gents, who was terrified of his male business partner, took to standing back and letting his Doberman Pincher take his seat. He smiled broadly when he told the class he hadn't been threatening or harsh toward his partner, he just used this metaphor to "bark" back when, in stark contrast, it had always been his tendency to retreat. How can you detach? Can you view yourself from the sidelines? Can you pretend to be someone who you admire for strength and courage? There is no right or wrong. Just as with the other exercises, it's just a matter of choosing what works for *you*. I knew a Fast Special Forces Trooper who told me he imagined himself as John Wayne whenever he prepared to go into battle (a tense meeting). Explore as many possibilities as you wish. There is no limit.

With the Four Step and now the added Six Steps of the Fast addendum to fall back on, you should be fairly well-equipped to become Fast On Your Feet even during the most contentious of confrontations.

To review:

- Step #1: Analyze what it is that stops you cold. (Humiliation? Anger?)
- Step #2: Stay in your groove. (Keep that rhythm flowing.)
- Step #3: Power through the obstacles with mental force. (Don't back down.)
- Step #4: Intentionally put yourself in grave danger conversationally. (Just for practice.)
- Step #5: Play the My Stance game. (Decide on what position you will take.)
- Step #6: Detach. (Remove yourself from the trauma at hand.)

184

Do each of the homework assignments I laid out for each Step and do them religiously. Your goal should be to make the process fun, too. Nothing worse than homework that is drudgery!

Reaching deep into the Fast Bag, I reminded this Special Forces class that one of the first drills we had done (Chapter Three) would be most helpful: Making the list of what was important in one's life and what was not so important. So I want you to start there, too. Revisit your original list and feel free to add to it. This alone will help you get a proper perspective. Realize that most negative and confrontational scenes, in which we are involved, are not life and death matters and that in our own individual big picture they have no real significance. This can be a great starting point in letting go and putting the bad scene behind us.

MORE STEPS

Notwithstanding the above, I also offered stay-after-Fasters even more ways to let go of a bad scene (soon after it takes place) because I realized this was also an integral part of the class's addendum. I introduced the need for additional ideas to the group early on and asked them to keep a journal of potential suggestions—ones they could share with the rest of the class when it became time to address that lesson. All recommendations, I instructed, were to be offered with the objective of dismissing the situation—erasing the discomfort of it—and making it seem less important than first thought. Such suggestions had to be viable ones that would allow the zombies to sleep at night and the bingers to stop overindulging. The broad cross-section of ideas were not only viable, many were downright practical. When it came time for each student to present his and her suggestions, it proved to be the highlight of the extra Fast course workshop. There were even those ideas that made all of us laugh out loud.

KICKING THE BAD HABITS

The following were just a handful of those that I collected and all proved to really work:

- Every time you start to recall the negatives of the situation **distract yourself** by reading, watching a movie, doing a crossword puzzle, playing chess or bridge, anything that forces your mind to put its attention elsewhere. What do I do? I either go shopping or I write! Nothing pulls me out of a funk faster! How about some of my students? They ranged from reading sections of the encyclopedia to watching "I Love Lucy" reruns.

- Call a friend or trusted colleague and **vent**. This is a healthy way to release the tension. I had one female student tell the class very proudly, "When you do call someone to vent, pretend that with every word, every exhale, you're expelling all the negative energy you took with you from the bad event. When you've run out of words (and steam) you will feel a sort of cleansing." She stood when she said this and then gently eased herself peacefully back into her chair. (Her bad trip was with a coworker who had been nice to her face, but vicious behind her back. She finally confronted her and the sparks flew.) I had yet another student who made his best friend pretend to be the bad guy during a phone conversation. They hung up. The friend called him back shortly after and my student told him off. My student and his friend had a hearty laugh over a beer later that week.

- Make a **list** of all the **positive scenes** in which you were engaged two hours before your negative, confrontational situation took place, and two hours afterwards. Keep playing back all those great moments as you become tempted to slip and obsess on that one bad moment (scene). This particular recommended strategy came from a 30-something male Fast student who went so far as to type out word-for-word the good scenes on his computer. He said doing so not only kept his perspective in tact, it also forced him to consciously focus on his computer screen and the words he was putting on it. He was smug when he shared this idea and appropriately so. We all cheered him.

- **Itemize** the things you **don't like about the person** with whom you have had the confrontation. (Shred the list so it doesn't get into the wrong hands.) When a young female Fast recruit shared this idea, she confessed that she saved one paragraph—the one she read out loud to the rest of the class. Though no names were mentioned (it was a rule I set forth), we did learn a lot about her female supervisor's double chin.

- Post the **person's picture** (or persons) or likeness (you can draw it yourself) on **a dartboard** and **aim for the bulls-eye**. This is just one more way to vent anger or frustration. When a burly 50ish student, Russell, offered this solution, the class erupted in a burst of laughter. The mirth quickly subsided however when Russ declared, "Well, I figured it was better than taking my .22 to work and blasting him out of his chair!" I immediately referred Russell to a therapist I knew who was good with anger management.

- I suggested Aretha Franklin earlier and here's another reason. Forget the background vocals this time. **Sing** the main part this time to **"Respect," loudly.** Actually, any kind of singing is great for losing the blues or dispensing negative energy that has been pent up. "What's yours?" I said as I went around the room and asked each student what song would be his or her anthem. We got everything from "Blue Skies" to "You Can Take This Job and Shove It." Lots of laughs, especially when someone hollered out "Stone Soul Picnic." None of us quite got the connection, but we applauded him anyway. One student, who worked for a snappy-mouthed engineer, went so far with this assignment as to buy himself a Karaoke machine. Big applause for him.

- **Role play** with a friend and do a bad scene reenactment (like the two guys on the phone), only this time say all the things you wished you had said or say things you should never say. My Special Forces Troopers and I spent an entire day on this exercise. It was wonderfully cathartic because each person finally got the chance to say what he or she wished they had said in that moment of confrontation (though it had to fall within the guidelines of what was appropriate). Some wanted to do their scenes more than once, often redoing the endings, so we did!

- **Buy yourself a present**—a reward for living through the situation. I remember the day a former boss took credit for a PR campaign idea I had presented to him the night before. This took place in front of the ad agency's client. I went out and bought myself a new dress, shoes to go with it and a new watch.

- Set an alarm. Give yourself a **prescribed amount of time** to obsess or dwell on the situation and when the alarm sounds, your time to do so will be up. A shy, female student rose to tell the class that she gave herself no more than two hours to ruminate over an upsetting workplace scene and when the buzzer sounded she made herself do something more meaningful and productive. She wrote poetry, she said. She admitted that it had been hard at first to assign a time limit to her upset, but after awhile she had programmed herself to adhere to this strict guideline. While in the throes of the *time zone*, though, she said she really obsessed on the situation. She was one of the nonsleepers and found this remedy to be a God-send. At first, when she awoke in the middle of the night, she used an hourglass to time herself out. "Now I only allow myself 15 minutes to stay fixated on a bad scene," she said proudly.

- Do some **rigorous physical activity** to rid yourself of the pent-up energy that frustration and anger can provoke. Don't restrict yourself to jogging, pounding a punching bag, skipping rope or any other form of predictable exercise. When it became his turn, one Faster jumped out of his seat to announce that he polished all his shoes, 20 pair, one right after another. (I wanted to invite him over!) Said he did so with gusto and speed. He also told the class that he was so tired afterwards that he slept like a baby. He was also one of my insomniacs.

- **Start looking** for a **new job,** new account, or whatever is appropriate in your circumstance to replace the situation and the person with whom you have had the confrontation. I had a student who went out and landed three new accounts to replace the existing one that made her life so miserable. She didn't need to subject herself to a client that always made a scene, even though he paid well. She loathed those moment with him when she never had a fast comeback for his insults. Letting go of her bad moments allowed her to latch on to brighter prospects. She said it also helped her sleep at night.

- **Familiar remedies to help you sleep** such as a glass of warm milk, a soothing meditation tape, a Yoga workout, a cup of chamomile tea, a hot bath, or a soak in a Jacuzzi are also good, old-fashioned remedies that help many people unwind after a stressful workday. One of the most hilarious moments in our sharing session of what helped the others sleep at night came from Harold, a 60-something banker, who was plagued with insomnia by a female bank manager who played passive-aggressive games with him. He said each time he tried to confront her she gave him the *who, me?* response, and it was keeping him up all night. He finally took to sleeping in his Jacuzzi since it was the only place he could comfortably conk out. Even though he reduced the water's temperature, his skin was suffering from the effects of soaking for six hours at a stretch. We affectionately dubbed him Hot-Tub Harry. I coach him often and still call him that!

- Another solution for sleeping well at night and one that rounded out our sharing session: **Count sheep.** I had one proud student who was up to 25,200 sheep in one night. He said he would rather have done that than think about the horrible scene that had taken place at his warehouse that day. One of his assembly workers actually spit on him in a fit of anger. He was afraid of responding in any other way than to fire him on the spot and have him escorted to the exit for fear of leaving himself open to a lawsuit. He was so rattled by the confrontation that he couldn't speak and later couldn't sleep.

STEP RIGHT UP

Now it's your turn to conjure up remedies that will help you let go of a bad scene and help you sleep at night (if that is a problem for you) or keep you from falling into the trap of overdoing. If you don't succeed with some of them, don't despair; try others. Each of us has positive triggers that will distract us from feeling bad (mine is hanging out with one of my children or talking to them on the phone or playing with one of my grandchildren). Whatever your buttons, they should keep you from destructive indulgences and help you get a decent amount of nighttime rest.

In the end, all these homework assignments are meant to help you be less flustered as you find yourself under the confrontational gun. Obviously if you're less flustered, you leave the door wide open to being for more fast on your feet.

Let's move on to our last chapter where I'll share with you snippets of several difficult situations and how they played out. All of them are culled from numerous Fast classes where students shared their less-than-fast experiences with the rest of the class. Each example covers the encounter, how they initially resolved the situation and how they wish they had resolved it or finally did. Some of these samples also include suggestions from fellow classmates as to how they would have handled the scene.

"Geez, why didn't you come to my defense this morning? You're an idiot ... a jerk..."

Chapter Eight

WALKING THE TALK:
Before And After
Examples Of Stepping On, Stepping In
And Stepping Up

As I round up and finish off your Fast lessons, I thought it might be fun reading to approach this last chapter in the same *screenplay* fashion that I've used to present various scenarios throughout the book. Just as in previous scenes, I've given each sketch a title and changed the names of the characters to protect both the guilty and the innocent. I've also changed many elements of the real situations so as not to embarrass any high-profile Fortune 500s depicted in them. As I mentioned at the close of the previous chapter, I will provide *playback* of each of these scenes based on class input and some of my own ideas. For homework, feel free to put your own spin on each scene.

<u>UP ALONG THE BOARD WALK – TAKE ONE</u>

INT. BLANKSHIP PHARMACEUTICALS -- REPORT-TO-THE-BOARD DAY

FADE IN:

Aerial view of cookie cutter glass-window-dominated high-rise. We plow through the roof, zooming downward, rapidly, where we see identical cubicles predictably arranged floor after floor, 24, 23, 22 ...until ...

We reach the boardroom tucked fashionably behind the lobby.

Tension is thick. No FDA approvals, yet 12 trustees are rapt, attentive. Reluctant Ralph, his supervisor, Bungle-it Bucknell, stand before them, stare straight ahead. Sixty solid seconds of dead silence, then ...

BOARD CHEESE CRAVITT

I said... we got the thumbs up on the GS-Flib 320 ... the Ambitril, right gentleman?

RALPH
(More dead air. It's not his turn)

Ralph's memory reverts to prep talk with Bucknell. Bucknell agreed to handle this question.

BUNGLE-IT BUCKNELL

Well, I guess (clears throat) I'll let Ralph field that question.

(Looks at Ralph)

RALPH
(Feeling screwed. Has nothing. Stares blankly)

Well, you see ...

BOARD CHEESE CRAVITT

What's going on here, gentleman? FDA approved us, right?

Bungle-it looks at Ralph. Like the Cheeses, he waits, expectant.

RALPH
(Ashamed)

Not exactly.

Deep groans all around from the other Cheeses. Board Cheese Cravitt now speechless. Bungle-it Bucknell and Reluctant Ralph just as quiet. Finally ...

BUNGLE-IT BUCKNELL

Tell them, Ralph.

RALPH

They turned us down.

Another round of groans, only louder.

PUSH PAUSE BUTTON

We've all been in Ralph's shoes. High stakes. Major pressure. Standing in a spotlight you don't want to be in. Assuming someone else will speak up, as they promised. Ralph counted on Bucknell. Then there he was, left to take the heat and forced to give the bad news.

No doubt Ralph wanted to throttle Bucknell, but how could he? Angry, he felt helplessly responsible to carry the ball. Did he kick himself around the block for not punting the responsibility back to Bucknell? Yes. Was Ralph made to feel like a fool? Yes. Could he have saved the moment? Perhaps. Could he have vamped? Probably. Could he have put a positive spin on the bad news? Possibly. At least that's what many in the class said as they studied the snippet playback more than once.

I did what I always do during this part of the class: I asked my students what they would have done. One student went off angrily bashing Bucknell. Don't go there, I chided. Sure you've got a legitimate beef, but that's not the point. That's what often trips people up in the midst of such jams: A preoccupation with pointing a finger rather than solving the problem *fast*. I redirected the class, asking them to throw out solutions, ones that would satisfy the situation and offer Ralph a Fast-On-Your-Feet Win.

We ran the scene several different ways.

Here are some of the more light-hearted suggestions that were initially tossed out:

- Feign a coughing fit, leaving Bucknell no choice but to stand and face the music alone

- Another had Ralph vehemently insist to Bucknell, "No, you tell them."

- One recommended Ralph dash for the fire alarm after asking, "Anyone else smell smoke?"

- Another suggested Ralph act surprised: "What? I thought you already knew, gentlemen …"

- Tell a big white lie. The suggestion was that Ralph grab for his ostensibly vibrating cell phone, gasp at the alleged text message and announce, "My wife's in labor, excuse me, but I must leave."

After having a little more fun with the scene, we got down to some serious work. The ultimate consensus right off the bat was that Ralph should have prepared himself with a My Stance strategy in the event Bucknell let him down. Everyone agreed that some preplanning could have circumvented Ralph's embarrassment. With stakes that high, the situation warranted some My Stance thinking, they said.

I complimented the class for its collective level head. After all, part of the Fast workshop message was to prepare for when you're least prepared and to expect the unexpected. Each of them had done well in getting that lesson down. Ralph was very frustrated over this situation, he told us, and so I tossed it back to the class. Now what?

Ralph was a good student, but had work to do. He had to make sure he wouldn't crumble the next time Bucknell pulled such a stunt. I asked him, along with the rest of the class, to rewrite the "Up Along the Boardwalk" script—picking up from Bucknell's line: "I'll let Ralph field that question." They went through several drafts and the following is what they finally settled on.

UP ALONG THE BOARDWALK—TAKE TWO

BUNGLE-IT BUCKNELL

Well, I guess **(clears throat)** I'll let Ralph field that question.

(Looks at Ralph)

RALPH
(Feeling screwed. Has nothing, at first. Pins tight eye contact on Bungle-It)

Oh, I couldn't ... with all due respect gentlemen ...
since Mr. Bucknell worked so hard preparing the
report on this matter, I insist he share it with you. **(A
gentlemanly gesture)** Bucky?

There were two alternate approaches, both of which I believe also would have worked. By "worked," I mean taken Ralph off the hook (or if he had to stay on it) helped him save some face. The first approach (Take Three) is where he gladly steps up and takes full responsibility for the bad news; the second (Take Four) is where Ralph pulls a clever *fake* on Bucky. In either case, both would have served as Fast reflexes to what seemed to be a sluggish situation.

UP ALONG THE BOARDWALK – TAKE THREE

BUNGLE-IT BUCKNELL
Well, I guess **(clears throat)** I'll let Ralph field that question.

(Looks at Ralph)

RALPH
(No shame. Projecting voice confidently)

Gentlemen, I'm afraid we didn't get the FDA approval at our meeting in Washington last week, but let me tell you this: Based on *that* meeting we walked away with a clear understanding of what it *will* take to get that approval the *next* time around. Not only that, the FDA committee let us know how impressed it was with our clinical trial information and each of them said they looked forward to our next meeting and moving forward with our request for approval. I'd like to present, now, what it is we need to do before that next meeting. I'm sure that's what all of you **(points to Cheeses)** are anxious to hear about.

UP ALONG THE BOARD WALK – TAKE FOUR

BUNGLE IT BUCKNELL
Well, I guess **(clears throat)** I'll let Ralph field that question.

RALPH
(Smirking inwardly)

Okay, Bucky, but ... wait. Sorry, there were specifics I wanted to share on that very question, but I forgot my notes. **(Gentlemanly gesture in Bucky's direction)** Bucky, you go ahead.

With Take Three, Ralph saves the day by deflecting what could have been a negative first response. Stepping up, fast, he diverts the Cheeses' attention from what *has* happened to what *can* happen—all positive stuff. (It's very hard to refute positive energy or ideas, I always tell my students.) As glum as things may appear, if you come from an upbeat and can-do stance, the audience will very often gravitate toward the same direction. Positives tend to breed more positives; negative energy fosters more of the same.

I also tell my students to offer up two positives for every negative. By so doing, a person's mind tends to lean toward the weight of the sentiment. (That I learned, doing a great deal of crisis Public Relations for many years.)

If you'll notice, Take Three left no room for Cheese Groans—Ralph had moved rapidly right past ... well, the past, and took the Board immediately into the future. He made them think about what needed to be done to get to the next square with the FDA, all the while leaning toward good news; thus optimism.

Rather than wallow in or harp on what Bucky didn't do, and should have done, in the presence of the Cheese Brigade, this Ralph "Take" made both of them look good. Definitely the best route to take on a bad ride!

I often hear my students complain about how unfair a situation turned out and how that was all they could focus on at the time—the inequity of it all. Get past it, I tell them. It does you no good to play the who's right-who's wrong game at the time of the incident, or even afterwards. What counts is a *fast way out* and one that is beneficial all the way around. That way there will be no regrets. If you're one of those who can't sleep at night thrashing around as you rehash the scene, a positive approach is the only Fast strategy to nurture. Something else I share with my students when giving this lesson: When you habitually respond with positive information—even in the face of negative events—your mental muscles will become trained to respond in *only* a positive way. That is what all that arduous training is about with the improv actor; they continually work those mental muscles to strengthen and tone them to stimulate specific positive and *fast* reflexes.

Something else I want you to grasp onto: In the world of improv, it's always about the show, not anything else, including the occasional discord that can occur among the actors when one of them pulls a Bucky and throws his *Division of Responsibility* (where every actor takes equal responsibility for the out come) to the other guy. Under all circumstances the show must go on, whether that's on the improv comedy stage or in the corporate boardroom. So no matter whose job it may be, improv actors must cover for another actor even if they don't really want to or don't find it fair to be forced to.

The cop-out option in Take Four—faking Bucky out—with an innocent "you better take the ball I forgot my gear," was not my choice of how to handle the situation. As my Special Forces Troopers pointed out though (they were getting really assertive and spunky after a few sessions), it was still a *Fast* response that would have spared Ralph any pressure, embarrassment or responsibility. They were right to suggest it and under certain circumstances the *Great Fake-out* might be just the ticket. Then again, every situation is different and we have to make our own personal judgment calls. My choice for Ralph was to opt for keeping the decorum. Better to have one of them step up instead of neither of them! Better to have Ralph cover for Bucky than to step on him.

As you've probably already guessed, I want you to write down several other choices as to what you would have said or done had you been walking in Reluctant Ralph's shoes. Take it from Bucky's line: "I'll let Ralph field that question." Be creative. Go with your impulses and instincts. Use your intuition. *Think fast!*

BANK ON THIS!—TAKE ONE

INT. SERVES-YOU-RIGHT BANK, PHONE BANK – CUSTOMER SERVICE CALL

(Nearing the end of her shift, Monica on headset. She yawns. Takes next call)

MONICA
(Pleasantly)

Good afternoon, it's a good day at Serves You Right. How may I serve you?

ANGRY CALLER

(Cynical snicker under heavy breath, then hollering)

I'll tell you how you can serve me! You can make good on my checks ...

Fast forward to just after information-gathering by Monica from Angry Caller

MONICA

(Struggling for patience)
It won't help if you yell at me, sir.

ANGRY CALLER

Well, how would *you* feel? You bounced three of my checks today and one of them was my house payment **(expletive, expletive!)**.

MONICA

But sir, you didn't have the funds to cover those checks.

ANGRY CALLER

Funds? *Funds?*

MONICA
(Rolling eyes)

Yes. Funds.

ANGRY CALLER
(Fuming)

What the *hell* kind of bank is this?

MONICA

Well, it's ... it's ...

HIT PAUSE:

Poor Monica. She was stumped. It was late. She was tired. Like the rest of us, exhaustion had taken its toll, making her more susceptible to brain freeze and far more vulnerable to the old *pause-and-hesitate*. Understandably so, Monica had handled irate customers all day. She knew perfectly well what kind of bank it was when Angry Caller asked. It was just that she found it hard to pull up the right response on the spot. She'd had her fill of Angry Callers for the day! She wasn't sure the answer she wanted to blurt out would be the appropriate one.

Monica was a Fast student who, in class, had asked to work on her penchant for giving into her mental fatigue, which was usually caused by her physical fatigue. She wanted to be able to remain consistently strong, even when she felt droopy from a grueling day and was faced with one more Angry Caller. Over-commit, I instructed, especially when you have the urge to slink back, when all you want to do is shrink away from the discord. Over-commit means to draw on that extra energy surge that is deep within all of us when we are brave and resolved enough to tap into it.

Naturally, we tossed Monica's less-than-Fast dilemma around the room and here were some immediate, quick-witted suggestions that came bouncing back:

- Vamp (stretch the dialogue—ad-lib). Pretend she couldn't hear the caller for a moment. "Keep gabbing," one student offered, until she could compose herself and decide on an appropriate response.

- Try a humorous approach. "Well I guess now would not be the best time to ask for a donation for the bank's latest cause, The Boys and Girls Club, would it Mr._____ (Angry Caller)?

- Commiserate: "I know how you feel. I hate when that happens."

- Meet him on his own turf: "Mr. (Angry Caller), please don't use profanity with me. And, please don't yell at me. I'm not paid to take abuse, just your call. I want to help. Now, can we start over?

I liked all of these ideas and told my class I was very proud of their freewheeling creativity. The enthusiasm to put to use their newfound communication Fast tools was really beginning to pay off.

The high point for me as we wrapped up suggested responses for Monica was:

ANGRY CALLER

What the *hell* kind of bank is this?

MONICA
(Skipping not one beat)

Serves you Right (**short pause**) Bank.

You have probably been in Monica's shoes—taking a call and having the person on the other end be in a horrible mood and take it out on you. So don't forget your homework with this scene; it's just great exercise for your brain!

Let's move on now to another scene where the confronter flung a far more personal attack at his subject.

This scene took place in an elevator. Mark, a Fast student, explained to the class that he was politely holding open the elevator door with a quick shove of his foot (his hands were full of files) to assist the arm that had reached around from the hallway side of the elevator in an attempt to keep the door from closing. At first he didn't realize the hand belonged to Bailey, a co-worker. The two were in a meeting that very morning in which Bailey was chastised for not having the required documentation completed; data he was asked to bring to back up his sales report. Mark and Bailey were counterparts. There always seemed to be friction between them. Mark frequently made a point of avoiding Bailey.

No sooner did the elevator door close when Bailey went off on Mark. Here's Take One of that scene:

FOOT IN THE DOOR – TAKE ONE

INT. EXPRESS ELEVATOR – DYNATECH SALES – 47TH FLOOR

BAILEY
(Shoots a quick nod of thanks to Mark. Suddenly realizes who it is. Scowls at him)

Well, thanks for nothing, Mark. Geez, why didn't you come to my defense this morning? You're an idiot … a jerk, and just wait until your ass is on the line. You think I'm going to be there for you? Think I'm gonna bail you out? Don't count on it, pal. I can't believe you did that to me! *Why*? Why would you do that to me? You're a moron. A total bonehead and I can't believe I have to work with you!

MARK
(Embarrassed. Humiliated. Stunned. Speechless)

Ah … I … uh …

BAILEY
(Visible disgust turns to sarcasm)

Oh, excuse me. Were you going to *say* something?

BAILEY
(Opens his mouth. Nothing comes out)

PUSH STOP ON YOUR MENTAL VCR:

Talk about getting stepped on! This truly is one of those situations that typically causes one's mental muscles to fold up and collapse. To be humiliated, especially in the presence of others, can leave a person shocked and tongue-tied. Mark was furious after the fact, he told us. Enraged. But more at himself for not having met the confrontation head on. He confessed that he had lain awake several nights afterwards hashing it over.

I felt sorry for Mark. The whole class did. We could relate.

Prior to taking suggestions for how he could have handled the circumstances, I reminded my students that if each of them would continuously work at toning his and her mental muscles and keep them pliable and fluid, they would never find themselves in the same bind as that of Mark. It's the repetition, the rehearsal, the constant drills that equip any one of us to jump right on top of any confrontation and face it head on. Don't forget what I said about using your instincts, impulses and intuition in confrontations. Lean on them, I said. I finished up my remarks by telling the class that taking on a confronter didn't mean coming back at them in a hostile manner, either. It just means that you have a response in the now, not later when you wish to kick yourself around the block for remaining silent. But since every situation is different, one has to know when to speak up and when it is appropriate to remain silent.

In the Bailey/Mark incident, according to the class and Mark, it would have behooved him to respond. Don't ever aggravate the aggressor if you think you're in danger, for example, losing your job or being at physical risk! But otherwise, speak up!

You can only imagine what a field day my class had with this scene! Some were mad enough to turn over cars! All agreed that even though Mark was virtually cornered in an elevator, he should never have stood by and allowed Bailey to get that far into his face. When polled, each student said Mark should have stopped Bailey at "thanks for nothing." Easier said than done, I admonished, especially when you can't see the harangue coming. I asked each of them to share his and her personal situations similar to Mark's. When they were done they were admittedly a little more humble. Most confessed they had also stood mute in the midst of confrontation, some on more than one occasion.

As they hunkered down to present Mark with some viable comebacks, they had great fun bouncing ideas off one another. Some made us laugh, others prompted applause. Before we get into the retakes, here are a few urgings that were made by Mark's classroom peers:

- Fake hearing loss: Say to Bailey. "Huh? What? Sorry, I had ear surgery not long ago and my hearing isn't fully restored. "Did you say something?"

- Take on a parental demeanor. "Hey, slow down Bailey. You get any more excited and you're gonna hurt yourself."

- Shut him out. Open up one of the files and begin intently reading it. Say nothing. Smile courteously at him, though, when exiting the elevator.

- Get off the elevator. Push the button for the next available floor and exit as soon as the door opens. Don't look back.

Naturally, we also took the time to rewrite the "Foot in the Door" scene, coming at it from a number of different angles. While the class turned in a slew of fantastic rewrites, the following two takes are the ones I picked to include in this passage. I think they were probably the most plausible of all the choices.

FOOT IN THE DOOR—TAKE TWO

BAILEY
(Shoots a quick nod of thanks to Mark. Suddenly realizes who it is. Scowls at him).

Well, thanks for nothing, Mark. Why didn't you come to my defense this morning? You're an...

MARK
(Locked and loaded. Cuts him off. Curt, but kind)

Come to your *defense*? Hey, pal, sorry you got dressed down, but maybe you should prepare the way we've all been asked to do. I know you're upset, but don't lay your blame at my doorstep. The responsibility for what happened lies with you.

WALKING ON EGGSHELLS

Though we have no way of knowing whether or not Mark's response in Take Two would have brought the conversation to a halt or incited more rage, I'm relatively confident this particular approach may have changed the course of Bailey's side of the conversation. Very often, when we let someone know immediately *(fast)*, that we will not allow them to fault us for their mistakes, they tend to back off. Had Bailey continued his diatribe, Mark could have chosen to stop Bailey again by saying something else along the same lines as his first response to Bailey. When Mark said nothing, it opened the door for Bailey to continue to verbally pound him. It is often the lack of response or the slowness of one that gets each of us into trouble. Remember your goal at all times: To be *fast on your feet*!

Let's rewind the scene between Bailey and Mark, once again, and try yet one more option.

<u>FOOT IN THE DOOR—TAKE THREE</u>

BAILEY
(Shoots a quick nod of thanks to Mark. Realizes who it is. Scowls at him)

Well, thanks for nothing, Mark. Geez, why didn't you come to my defense? You're an idiot … a jerk, and just wait until your ass is on the line. You think I'm going to be there for you? Think I'm gonna bail you out? Don't count on it buddy. **(Angrier)** I can't believe you did that to me! Hung me out to dry! *Why?* Why would you do that to me? You're an idiot. A total bonehead and I can't believe I have to work with you!

MARK
(Bursts into laughter. Offhandedly pushes button to get off at the nearest floor)

"Oh, Bailey, I swear. You're a riot, man! That's funny. *Really* funny!"

(Doors open. Mark exits, tossing remaining laughter over his shoulder. Doors close)

BAILEY
(Stumped. Mouth agape)

Take Three was a rather unique choice, but one the class voted on as their second pick for how Mark could have handled Bailey. He didn't let Bailey get to him. Instead, he behaved as though he found Bailey's comments absurdly funny. He also was clever and thinking *fast* by nonchalantly pressing a selection on the elevator button panel at the outset of his quick response. Delivering the final line and being the first to exit gave Mark the upper hand. It would have been virtually impossible for Bailey to attack Mark further because the elevator doors would have closed and Mark would have literally left the scene.

Also, when we laugh off a verbal attack, the attack suddenly loses its punch. In fact, it somehow ricochets back at the attacker leaving him feeling embarrassed, bewildered, even foolish. It's akin to laughing lovingly at a child who is throwing a tantrum.

All agreed that Takes Two and Three offered Mark a chance to save face in the midst of a difficult situation. You're right, I told them. They were both plausible options, but once again the point is to make either of those choices, or another appropriate one, *rapidly, without skipping a beat*. Therein lays the heart of the victory: To maintain poise and presence and offer up a viable reply with no hesitation.

It's now up to you to concoct some Takes of your own. How would you have handled Bailey if you were in Mark's shoes? Write down at least four potential reactions and/or responses to Bailey's diatribe. Come at this assignment with your voice and style, and above all keep your responses appropriate. Stay away from choices that return the attack. It just cheapens your style. Don't forget all the earlier guidelines in the Fast Lesson Plan that I covered in previous chapters. Review them, if need be, before doing this assignment.

SCENE THIS!

This particular scene depicted one of those classic situations where Hoagy (the main character) couldn't keep his client on point. When Barney asked for something—information from vendor Hoagy—he constantly cut poor Hoagy off or, as you will see, changed the subject altogether. Hoagy announced that having a meeting with Barney was like trying to nail Jello to the wall. According to Hoagy, this frustrating situation didn't happen occasionally, but every single time he met with Barney. The only constant, he reported in summing up, was that Hoagy knew his client would come out of left field with something; he just never knew what that *something* would be. That drove him mad. Hoagy would leave every meeting downtrodden because he rarely got anything accomplished.

<u>ALL OVER THE PLACE—TAKE ONE</u>

INT. OFFICE OF THE VICE PRESIDENT – EARLY AFTERNOON -VNR COMMERCIAL OFFICE FURNITURE

(Barney greets Hoagy warmly with his usual hearty handshake. Hoagy sits. Barney smiles.)

BARNEY
(Smug)

Whatcha got?

HOAGY
(Hopeful)

Well last time we met you indicated **(slight nervous laugh)** that you were interested in our new line of automatic retractable filing cabinets. So, I brought the new catalogue with …

BARNEY
(Looks toward the window)

I don't understand women, Hoag. They always get mad at
'cha for nothin'.

HOAGY
(Trying for rapport at any cost)

Well, I know how that is. Just last week my wife blew up at
me because I left my socks on the floor, even though I've been
doing it for years, and I asked her …

BARNEY
(Furrows brow. Looks through Hoagy)

Did my secretary ask you to bring …

HOAGY
(Waits. Looks at Barney patiently, politely, expectantly)

BARNEY
(Gets an amused look on his face)

I think it's high time I ordered some lobby furniture, Hoag.

HOAGY
(Shuffles through briefcase pulls out chair, sofa catalogues)
We've got some really good sales going on for leather sofas …

BARNEY
(Starts to giggle)

I was thinkin' about matchin' desks for the girls out front.
They're always dressin' like twins and I think it might be
funny to …

HOAGY
(Trades catalogues in his briefcase)

BARNEY
(Pensive)

Say, who's the highest paid player in the NBA, do ya know? I got a hundred bucks on Shaq. Am I right?

HOAGY
(Trying to keep up)

I think it's …

BARNEY
(Distracted)

Would love to see what you've got in those **(points to the mess on Hoagy's lap)**, but I gotta jam. Have a meeting at Ronco in 20 minutes. Gotta hurry. Need to be back here for a meeting in two hours.

HOAGY
(Apologetic)

Sorry. Should I … could I … want me to come back …?

BARNEY
(Stands to usher Hoagy out)

I'll call ya …

PUSH PAUSE

Needless to say, Hoagy felt demoralized. He also told the class that he began to break into a sweat each time he pulled up at VNR because he never knew if he would make a Barney sale, have to try to *sneak* in a Barney sale, or waste his time and make *no* Barney sale. VNR, he told us, was his company's biggest account and the pressure was on for him to come back to the office with an order after every visit. His dilemma, he said, was that he just didn't know how to redirect his client or keep him on course to get the job done. The minute he thought of an appropriate response, Barney had left that particular idea behind and introduced something else. Most of the class sympathized with Hoagy. They too had experienced the same in their worlds of business.

In keeping with the format of the class, everyone threw in their two cents as to what Hoagy could do to and corral his client. Some of the wisecrack suggestions (I always encourage them to throw them on the table first to stimulate those Fast muscles) included the following:

- Walk Barney to the car and climb in the passenger side. Keep him captive until he buys, even if it means spending the afternoon at Ronco.
- Walk backwards to the office exit. Close the door. Stand against it. Take Barney hostage until he buys desk, sofa *and* chair.
- Fake a crying spell. Guilt him into buying something, anything, before he's able to walk out the door.
- Tell him you think, as you rise to leave the meeting, that while listening to the radio on the way over you thought you heard that Ronco had burned down.

You can probably guess that all of us in class had a few laughs over these suggestions! Very often in class, it's the laughter and the camaraderie this lesson segment produces that stimulates the mental juices and prompts the mental muscles to be free enough to come up with the real or more viable solutions.

The class agreed that Hoagy should set his sites on calling on those clients who were easier to communicate with. They also said better he develop new leads from referrals that were good accounts—ones that might replace the revenue derived from Barney—than to waste time with the Barneys of the business world. Great recommendations, I said, bursting into abrupt applause. But what about the scene as it came down? I wanted to know what they thought about how it had ended. How might it be rewritten or redirected? How can you change it so Hoagy is left feeling more productive and better about himself?

Again, we brainstormed like a tight-knit community of sketch writers until we settled on the following redo. We picked it up from the line:

BARNEY
(Gets an amused look on his face)

I think it's high time I ordered some lobby furniture, Hoag.

HOAGY
(Readily pulls out chair, sofa catalogues)

We've got some really good sales going on for leather sofas …

BARNEY
(Starts to giggle)

I was thinkin' about matchin' desks for the girls out front. They're always dressin' like twins and I think it might be funny to ...

HOAGY
(Trades catalogues in his briefcase)

BARNEY
(Pensive)

say, who's the highest paid player in the NBA, do ya know? I got a hundred bucks on Shaq. Am I right?

HOAGY
(Easily keeping up)

I got a hundred bucks in this coupon right here (**waves a piece of paper pulled quickly from his briefcase. It's really not a coupon; Hoagy pretends it is**) that says you get a big discount on the first desk ya buy. If ya buy it before I leave this office today.

BARNEY
(Not as distracted)

Coupon? Hundred bucks?

HOAGY
(Confident. Upbeat)

Hundred bucks and I'll tell ya what … I'll give you another fifty bucks off anything else you buy today.

BARNEY
(Scratches head)

I really gotta jam. Got a meeting at Ronco in 20 minutes. Gotta hurry. Gotta be back here for a meeting in two hours.

HOAGY
(Thinking Quickly)

How about I ride along with ya? I was going to drop off some brochures there anyway. You drive. I'll write up the order and have the paperwork all ready for you to sign before you can shove the car into park.

When I questioned the class about how Hoagy would get back to his car, almost the entire class on cue said, "Taxi." The class tossed around several solutions, all of which reflected *fast* reactions to Barney's sudden departure. One of the options they explored was to suggest that Hoagy fib and say he had met Shaq O'Neill and would be glad to tell Barney all about it if only he had time (thus luring him into more time). I agreed with them that sticking by Barney's side was quite possibly a smart choice. I did gently tell the student who suggested the Shaq fib that lying is not necessarily a good idea. You can trap yourself, I told him. And then if you're found out, there goes the trust factor. Stretching the truth or expounding on a compelling idea that might keep a client's interest is not at all a bad idea, especially if you're trying to extend the meeting and create an opportunity to make a sale. When this guy asked for an example with regard to that point I said, well, what if Hoagy quickly thought to say that he'd heard Shaq was the highest paid basketball player to date and had also heard that he bought such and such with his money and his biggest luxury was this and that. Such fodder would have filled nicely and been a fast response when that zinger came at Hoagy.

Which brings me to a very important principle I teach all my Fast students and my improvisational comedy students: Read newspapers and magazines daily and watch the news, too. Many of us are caught in binds like that of Hoagy where, if only he had been more abreast of day-to-day events and news items, he may have had something meaningful and substantive to quickly toss back about Shaq. For the improv player it's imperative that they know *daily* and almost *hourly* what is going on in the world. They have no idea what an audience member will ask of them when they hit the stage. It truly discredits them if they demonstrate that they can't act upon a suggestion because they just don't know what news item the audience member is referring to. Same goes for each of us business professionals. We should be in the know just in case we need to react quickly to a remark like the one Barney threw out for which Hoagy had no response. People in general, I have found, find us far more interesting and capable when they see that we are abreast of the goings on in the world or community.

I explained to my class, as we sat around discussing the Hoagy mishap, that when you're well read and broadcast or Internet savvy, you stand a much better chance of carrying on a conversation when someone suddenly throws a zinger out of nowhere.

In the end, all agreed that hanging in there and finding a good excuse to stay with Barney would give him more time to make the sale. Perhaps Barney would not have purchased anything, but at least (according to the collective vote of the class) he had a better chance of getting Barney to do so. They also felt that Hoagy would have garnered more respect from Barney by not reacting the way he had when Barney said he had to leave for the Ronco meeting. If you recall, Hoagy asked: "Should I ... could I

…Want me to come back?" Desperation is a funny thing; in any form, it turns people off.

Afterwards, the class and I huddled with Hoagy. He agreed to keep his eye on the news and vowed not to allow Barney or anyone else to fluff him off. He said he would aim toward having a rapid reply for all comments thrown at him; especially the ones that would no doubt come out of nowhere.

I'm asking you to do the same as what was asked of Hoagy. Refuse to be defeated. If the meeting is over, it's over; but that doesn't mean you can't leave it on a high note. There is no reason why you should be left feeling impotent or at a loss for carrying on a topical conversation when it comes time to sell your wares (wares could be an idea or a point of view). Remember the Fast goal: To never be at a loss for words!

CLOSING SCENE
PROMPTER HELL—TAKE ONE

EARLY MORNING – LAUNCH OF THE NEW CREOLE CONVERTIBLE.
DEALER'S MEETING

FULL FRAME:
Huge convention center ballroom. Camera one pans clusters of expectant audience members, 4000 dealers, all chatting animatedly. Piped in music overhead is loud, they're yelling to hear one another. Suddenly, big drum roll. Camera two, tight shot on big shots, back stage. Speech coach giving last-minute instructions to speakers. They straighten ties. High fives all around, until …

Music fades.

V.O. And now ladies and gentlemen, please join me in welcoming the president of Marmoto Motors …
Johnnnnnnnnnn Blaaaaankenship …

Blankenship, big smile. Confidently strides across stage. Walks to point where stage hands have spiked his mark. Pauses, turns, looks ahead at center TelePrompter. Begins …

BLANKENSHIP

We've come a long way this past year in creating a new automobile for the upscale buyer, the type of buyer who is looking for luxury, comfort, and above all an affordable price in a sports car.

TelePrompter continues to scroll …

Today's car buyer is more knowledgeable about the car-buying process, more aware of what questions to ask, and knows exactly what kind of deal they expect. It isn't so much about …

Words on screen disappear. Monitor is black. Blankenship's eyes bulge. Face flushes.

BLANKENSHIP
(Slight, nervous laugh, recites last line from memory)

It isn't so much about … about … about …

Poor John Blankenship. There he stood, stripped of his speech-making dignity, completely dependent on technology to carry him through his talk. It was definitely one of those terrible moments that can be utterly horrifying to anyone in his shoes! Before thousands, a technical glitch had rendered Blankenship wordless. If only he had been trained in the Fast on your Feet principles he may have been able to continue without skipping a beat, whether the TelePrompter ever began to operate again or not.

Naturally, we kicked this situation around in class. Since this circumstance is quite different from those where a conversation is taking place between two or more people, it required different Fast solutions.

Or did it?

I asked the students for feedback and all said they believed there really was no major difference in Blankenship's dilemma compared to that of the many others I asked them to work through. He was stopped dead in his tracks. Not by something someone else said, but by a machine that had let him down.

One student finally summed it up: Being stumped is being stumped. Yep, I said. Okay, in that case, tell me what John *could have* done before 4,000 audience members to recoup?

Here's what they offered:

- Make a joke. Buy time. "Why don't we all have a cup of coffee while we wait for my speech to reappear? With 4,000 of you that means they could reinstall the entire system ... from scratch."

- Apologize. "I am so sorry ladies and gentlemen. Our TelePrompter seems to have failed us, and I must confess, I do rely on it. Again, I am sorry. Please wait just a moment ..."

- Opt for a back-up plan. "Forgive me while I grab my handwritten notes. I will use them to continue with my talk this morning until the crew can restore power. I appreciate your patience."

- Laugh. "Boy, I'll tell you. Nothing like the technology of the 21st century to get the day going." Most audiences will laugh *with* the speaker no matter what. I told you earlier: Your audience will always mirror you. Same goes for when you flub up and laugh at yourself.

- Turn it over to someone else: "Well, it's not about ... you know, I'm going to ask our product development guy to join me here on stage to tell you about today's driver and what it's *really* about ... Ladies and Gentlemen, Troy Briscoe ..."

- Prepare for a disaster! Yes, ask the stage hands ahead of time to prepare cue cards, just in case ...

Though many business people I coach don't memorize their speeches since they've come to rely on PowerPoint slides or TelePrompter support to carry them, I sternly tell them they must be ready for the worst case scenario. Always!

There is a trick I have taught many of my public speaking students and I share it with you now; those of you who are dependent on technology or visual aids to get you through your talk. It is called the Square-within-the-Square Theory. It's used to create and organize a speech. The illustration on the following page of the Square-within-the-Square Theory is what I often used early on when making my ExecuProv introductory speech, the one that explains how improv benefits the business professional.

The outside square is reserved for the central or overall theme of the speech. Inside that large square sits as many individual squares as needed to cover however many chunks of information are imparted in the overall speech. On each square, write down bullet points that fit within a topic of that square (chunk) of information covered beneath the umbrella idea or overall subject (outside square).

To keep your talk lively and interesting (I always tell my students it is contrast and variety that makes us interesting) try attaching a mood or frame of mind to each of the bullet points, as I have indicated in my speech. Also, to conclude each square (chunk) of information, I provide a punchline. A punchline does not mean you have to offer something humorous. It can be a quote your mother or coach once said to you, an anecdote, a story, a hard-hitting piece of philosophy ... the idea with the punchline is that, in a sound bite, it reiterates, sums up and/or encapsulates the overall message of each square. For example, in my third square "Other Skills," I typically get a few volunteers from the audience to do a listening exercise to demonstrate one of the points I really want to drive home. Notice that I have also attached minutes to each square in order to stay on track and on time.

"SQUARE WITHIN A SQUARE" EXAMPLE

Theme: Everyone Is A Performer, But Few People Are Trained To Be

(1-hour speech)

I. Intro

8 min.

- Execuprov is
- Born – *Friendly*
- Who Coach – *Story Telling*
- Stars – *Matter of Fact*
- Story (Punchline) – *Fun*

II. Basics

6 min.

- Breathing – *Free*
- Diction – *Firm*
- Concentration – *Mysterious*
- Awareness – *Pensive*
- Demo (Punchline)

III. Other Skills

18 min.

- Mental Agility – *Energetic*
- Energy – *Enthusiastic*
- Emotion – *Desperate*
- Listening – *Intense*
- Give & Take – *Patient*
- Refusal/Denial – *Concerned*
- Body Language – *Cynical*
- Timing/Spontaneity – *Upbeat*
- Story (Punchline) – *Fun*

IV. What's So Funny

8 min.

- Humor in Talks – *Serious*
- Gauge Audience – *Intellectual*
- Writing It – *Enthused*
- Delivery – *Funny*
- Homework – *Serious*
- Demo (Punchline)

V. Square within Square

10 min.

- Chart – *Matter of Fact*
- AP Story/Film – *Light*
- Jane, Dick, Spot – *Fun*
- 20 Min. – *Patient*
- Story (Punchline)

VI. Summary

10 min.

- Dos/Don'ts – *Compassionate*
- E.P. Classes – *Direct*
- Questions – *Friendly*
- Quote (Punchline)

Students of mine who use TelePrompTer or PowerPoint as a crutch, take 3x5 note cards with them to the podium and set them there or shove them inside their coat pocket for quick reference with the information for each square on each card. If Blankenship had used the Square-within-the-Square Theory it would have served him in two ways: First, he could have had them with him, pulled them out and kept going despite the teleprompter failure, and two, he could have used them to semi-memorize his speech beforehand. That's correct. When you divide your talk into chunks and jot down bullet points on each card (representing each inside square), it helps you to learn, separate and *retain* the information—it's a wonderful way to rehearse.

I coach many people shortly before a speech. Many of them defer to a TelePrompTer to carry them along, and sadly, most don't even know what it is they are saying as they're saying it. I insist they sit with me to go through their script and read it. Simultaneously they are asked to separate it by marking a line across the text that separates one idea from the next. This gets them in touch and familiar with the content. By writing out and compartmentalizing the information, it helps them get clarity on each section of the talk (the different ideas covered), and the important points the speaker is trying to make. With note cards in tow, a person can *improvise quickly* no matter what disaster befalls them!

If you're like Blankenship and use any technology such as a teleprompter, I strongly suggest you have a back-up plan. Know your material well enough to wing it, just in case.

During our Blankenship feedback session we had more suggestions than just those I listed. The funniest one was the guy who suggested Blankenship just walk off the stage.

He stood, pretending to play Blankenship, and said, "Well, in the words of Bugs Bunny ... That's all folks.'" Then he exited stage-left, very dramatically. We all thought it was amusing, but not very practical!

ENTER THE SCENE

I would like to ask now that you write some of your own scenes, the ones that didn't go so well, and the ones that you anticipate will cause you some difficulty in the future.

To make this assignment fun, try doing them in the same screenplay or sketch format that I have used throughout the book. Not only does that style make you focus on seeing the scene in total, including the environment in which it unfolds, but it also allows you to get the full impact of every word spoken. This exercise also serves to let you use your imagination to its fullest, in terms of descriptions of feelings, thoughts and perceptions (both your own and others). So make note of reactions, gestures, attitudes—those parenthetical descriptions we playwrights term stage directions. They, too, will more clearly point you in the right direction, for as I have discussed, often we need to respond to a person's body language or mood (subtext), not just the spoken word.

Take your time with each task.

Additionally, to challenge yourself, try several versions of the same scene. This will help you exercise your mental muscles more rigorously. Rigor, ironically, begets agility and the more sinuous your mind, the quicker you can respond. Finding alternates to the same scenario is wonderful practice. This is how good habits are formed.

Sometimes in class I ask my students to take one scene from a pivotal point and keep reworking the ending with several alternatives. Some endings may be more feasible or appropriate than others, but by doing this assignment my students were astounded at how many options were available to them to get the job done. As you do your scenes, I'm sure you will have the same experience.

This write-it-yourself exercise is also a fabulous way to deconstruct (then reconstruct) that tough moment you may not have been able to resolve before; the one that may still be nagging at you. I had one student who said it wasn't until she dissembled the run-in with her boss over who was supposed to have brought the Cherry Jubilee to the Cherry Jubilee-themed company picnic that she finally got in touch with what it is she *wanted* to say.

Here it is: "It was my understanding that I was commissioned to *organize* the Cherry Jubilee event, not make the actual dessert. Heck, consider yourself lucky, Mr. Bradford. My Cherry Jubilee looks like Strawberry Shortcake upside down!" Unfortunately, at the moment her boss asked her why it was she didn't bring the themed dessert, she had just stood there, mute.

If you don't want to rehash old scenes, start from scratch. Keep track of the new ones each day, shortly after they happen. Without too much pause, steal away for a moment and jot down (either in long hand or on your computer), all the makings of the scene, taking special note of where it was in the scene that you were caught off guard, when you choked or faltered. See if you can rework these scenes focusing on different responses on your part. Don't hesitate. Keep redoing the scene quickly. It will force you to utilize your new Fast kit. By doing your scenes over and over and coming up with different choices in rapid succession, you will both stretch and tone your mental muscles. The more you stretch them, of course, the more pliable they will become. (As a trigger, one student carries around a rubber band. She tells me the analogy is that the difference between a new rubber band and one that has been pulled over and over is similar to how her mental muscles have become from stretching and pulling at them. Nice and loose! As a reminder, she fiddles with the rubber band constantly.) Naturally, malleability means you'll increase your ability to fire off appropriate replies on the spot when next you're under the gun, or need the good *(quick)* sense to hold one back in the event it should be stayed.

There is no limit to how many scenes you should write and rewrite. That's strictly up to you. But, please, you must do them. This assignment is one of the best fast lessons of all!

As I leave you to your work, remember this: Every piece of communication is a scene and my wish is that after all your diligent effort you will feel comfortable and be forthcoming in each and *every* scene, and that you are able to feel confident that you will always have a fast response with little or no real thought preceding it, no matter what situation you are *unprepared for* or what *unexpected* circumstance or piece of communication comes your way.

Now, get out there in the workplace and start talking, *fast*!

Epilogue

Skipping Along: No Tripping or Slipping

Well, congratulations! You have just successfully completed a correspondence course in the Fast on Your Feet class! Let me compliment you for all your hard work and for doing all the assignments in this book! Many of them may have been uncomfortable, tedious and time-consuming, but I'm sure you'll agree, all of them were necessary.

In order to keep your mental muscles pliable and strong, you will need to keep working out. I know that most business professionals are very busy, but it is through repetition of the drills that you gain the skill you want and need to handle any communication situation.

Be mindful of:

- Letting go of your inhibition and fear. They have no place in your communication. Don't give in to either of them, ever. Generally, they are self-imposed. Tell yourself, *ah who cares.*

- Create a new mindset. Make your two lists: The things that are truly important and those things that simply are not.

- Listen to your intuition. Heed your instincts. Go with

your impulses. I'm not nearly as concerned about you saying the wrong thing as I am you hesitating and saying nothing at all. If you ascribe to all the lessons in this book, I rather doubt you will be one of those who ever puts his foot in his mouth.

- Practice the Four-Step, religiously. Like a ballroom dancer that takes to the floor regularly to master the footwork basics, do the same with your *mental feet.*

- Sense when to step forward, when to step back, and be quick to rebound when you have mistakenly or accidentally put your foot in your mouth. Don't just stand there, provide an appropriate comeback. You now know how!

- When it's necessary (among those who you suspect might be obdurate or challenging) flip the *Red Alert* switch to the *on* position and leave it there (think of your mental faculties like the crew that is always on standby at the firehouse). Always sit (or stand) tall. Project a strong and steady voice and, to buy time when you have to, ask questions. These extra tools, if you recall, are other Fast tricks that you can stash in your Fast bag.

- If you need them, take on the homework tasks spelled out in the Special Forces Fast on your Feet addendum. There are six steps to conquer: Analyze what it is that stops you cold in your verbal tracks; stay in your groove; power through obstacles with mental force; put yourself in grave communication danger to build strength and stamina; play the My Stance game; and detach. The last step in this Special Forces Fast lesson series alone might be just the ticket to keep you from cowering in the midst of those who confront you.

- Don't obsess over the negative scenes. Leave them behind you. Instead, dwell on those positive scenes when your communication worked. Build on your successes.

- Write out your scenes. The ones that didn't go so well and the imminent ones you dread. Of all the work assignments, I think this one is the most valuable, for the process takes a methodical approach and careful thought. You can't just rush through it. Writers will tell you that writing is all about rewriting. Getting a scene *just so* takes time and work. Go ahead and, for drill, write out the scenes that *did* work, too. They will reinforce for you what does work and also make you feel good about yourself! Part of the Fast lesson is to build self-esteem. Besides, writing the scenes down provides even more clarity. A thorough understanding of why communication went so well is also what you're after!

One last thing and one of the most important messages I wish to leave with you: Master the Fast techniques at *your own pace*. Some of the lessons may have seemed overwhelming to you and I suppose if you try to do them all at once, they certainly can be. Know that every improv comedy player (including me!) has spent weeks, months and even years getting their skill set firmly in place. "Little by little" and "Nice and easy" are two mantras I want you to keep saying to yourself. There is no magic number as to how many exercises you should do or how often, that's strictly up to you. That said, however, keep those mental muscles stimulated and moving for that's what keeps them sharp and flexible.

In addition to doing the assignments I've prescribed, choose some of your own. Join an improv class, engage in board games that are mentally challenging, play charades; take on any activity that deals with sheer mental creativity and/or demanding on-the-spot problem solving. Any activity that sparks spontaneous problem solving is what you're after to keep your mind fluid, alert and sharp.

Know that after enough challenges, enough victories, and after conditioning and reprogramming your mental muscles, you will always handle those difficult communication situations quickly, appropriately, and, of course, fast.

Most of all, be confident and comfortable knowing that because of all your hard work you will *never again* be one of those business professionals who stops dead in his or her verbal tracks, who is at a loss for words, whose mind goes blank—who doesn't know what to say when ....

About the Author

Cherie Kerr, who founded ExecuProv in 1983, has provided a variety of classes on presentation and communication skills to hundreds of business professionals from Fortune 100 and 500 companies. Her clients include BP America, Ericsson, Toyota, Kawasaki, Mitsubishi, Ingram Micro, Bank One, Delta Dental, Experian, Foothill Capital, PacifiCare, Allergan, Universal Studios, Fluor Corporation, 3i Implant, ConAgra Foods, The Hilton Hotel and Marriott Hotel Corporations, California Trucking Association, Office Max/Boise, Volcom, Nissan, Honda, Bank of America, BJ's Restaurant Brewhouse, Southern California Edison, Panasonic, Black & Decker and Office Depot, to name but a few.

Kerr has also provided a number of classes to various universities and collegiate departments including Chapman University; Otis College of Art and Design; University of Southern California; California State University, Fullerton; Vanguard University; University of California, Irvine, The Paul Merage School of Business; UCI Medical Center, Anesthesiology Department; the U.S. Naval Academy at Annapolis; and the U.S. Military Academy at West Point. She also has worked for a number of governmental agencies including the L.A. City Attorney's Office, the L.A. District Attorney's office, the County of Orange, the Orange County Bar Foundation and the Orange County Juvenile Drug Court Program. She is a certified Provider for the Continuing Legal Education Program for the State Bar of California, and has served as that organization's official speaker-trainer for its Board of Governors.

A founding member of the world-famous L.A. Groundlings, Kerr was the founder in 1990, Executive Producer and Artistic

227

Director for the Orange County Crazies, a sketch and improvisational comedy troupe in Santa Ana, California. She also served as the group's head writer. She has received rave reviews for her work as a writer, performer and director.

Kerr has taught improvisational comedy to actors since 1973, and teaches other classes as well, including a class on how to develop original characters and how to write sketch comedy. She has studied with some of the best improv and comedy teachers in the business, including Kerr's former scene partner, Gary Austin, founder of the L.A. Groundlings, and a former member of the highly acclaimed group, The Committee; Michael Gellman, a director and teacher for Second City, in Chicago; and Jeannie Berlin (an Academy Award nominee and Elaine May's daughter.) In her formative years, she studied at the Pasadena Academy of Drama with Eleanor Dopp.

A writer for more than 35 years, Kerr has owned an award-winning public relations firm since 1978, KerrPR, which offers public relations services to a variety of clients. She handles many crisis situations and is regarded as a prime source by media (such as Good Morning America, Entertainment Tonight, Larry King Live, CNN, 20/20, The Today Show, Anderson Cooper 360º, The Sunday Show, Nightline and many others) to provide them with expert sources for commentary.

Kerr has written, produced and directed an original full-scale musical comedy, written two full-length screenplays, 12 books, two screenplays and more than 400 comedy sketches; she is a member of ASCAP, and has been honored as an award-winning journalist and publicist. Kerr was named, along with Disney's Michael Eisner, as one of the "Top Ten Most Sensational People in Orange County" by Orange Coast Magazine. She has been quoted and featured in many publications including the OC Register, The Los Angeles Times, the Harvard Review Communication Newsletter, Forbes, American Way magazine, the Sacramento Bee, USA Today, The New York Times, Investor's Business Daily and The Associated Press, in addition to many others. She also did an AOL radio tour on email etiquette and has been featured on numerous websites.

Kerr is the mother of award-winning filmmaker, Drake Doremus, winner of the 2011 Sundance Film Festival U.S. Dramatic Competition award for Like Crazy, a fully improvised film (based on a 50-page outline and sold to Paramount Pictures for $4-million); Doremus trained under Kerr as a member of the OC Crazies sketch and improv troupe, having started on Kerr's stage at the age of six and leaving for school at the American Film Institute at age 19.

Kerr also starred in her own one-woman show, Out of Her Mind, which met with great success and which she single-handedly wrote. In it she played a number of original characters.

In addition to lecturing and teaching ExecuProv courses, both in classroom situations and in private, one-on-one coaching sessions, Kerr provides speechwriting services for many of her clients. Kerr also provides her creative services to large companies for corporate comedy industrials and also produces ExecuProv's Humorous Training Video Library, a diverse library of video spoofs designed to train the business professional in a fun and humorous way. Companies and individuals access the HTVL catalogue with a library card, which gives them rights to include the humorous videos in their presentations, adding that extra dash of humorous panache.

Another of Kerr's many endeavors, Ex-Serp Productions, ExecuProv's sister company, provides services as a media consulting firm and production company specializing in the development of documentary television programming, Internet commercial webisodes and public service announcements.

Kerr is frequently sought out as a keynote speaker addressing presentation and communication skills and humor in the workplace, and is also available for speaking engagements.

Cherie Kerr resides in Santa Ana, California. She is the mother of three and also has five grandchildren.

ExecuProv offers workshop sessions, seminars and private coaching to both companies and individuals world wide. Ms. Kerr is available for keynote speeches and special appearances. Please submit a written request for any of the above to:

ExecuProv
DePietro Performance Center
809 N. Main Street
Santa Ana, CA 92701

Email: CherieKerr@aol.com
Visit ExecuProv's website: www.execuprov

Other Books By Cherie Kerr

The Bliss or "Diss" Connection?
il Etiquette For The Business Professional

Funny Business:
b Make <u>You</u> Laugh On The Job Every Day

Miller to Say a Few Words" —*New and Exciting Ways to Improve Speaking and Presentation Skills Through the Use of Improvisational Comedy Techniques*
Foreword by Phil Hartman

"What's So Funny?" —*How to Get Good Storytelling and Humor Into Your Speeches and Presentations*

"When I Say This...," "Do You Mean That?" — *Enhancing On-The-Job Communications Skills Using the Rules and Tools of The Improv Comedy Player*
Foreword by Julia Sweeney

Death By Powerpoint:
How To Avoid Killing Your Presentation and Sucking the Life Out of Your Audience

Build to Laugh:
How To Construct Sketch Comedy With The Fast and Funny Formula

Charlie's Notes: A Memoir

I would like to order the following books:

_____

_____

Name _____

Address _____

City _____

State _____ Zip _____

Telephone No. _____ Fax No. _____

Email Address _____

Credit Card   ❏ Visa   ❏ MasterCard

Credit Card No. _____

Expiration Date _____

Signature _____

Please put me on your email list to be informed of upco classes held at the DePietro Performance Center

Please mail orders forms to: ExecuProv Press, 809 N. Main Street, Santa Ana, CA 92701

Kerr's books are also available at Amazon.com, Barnes & Noble.com and at all major bookstores throughout the country